Petite, Pretty & Piped

60 Delicate Cupcakes & Mini Cakes to Satisfy Every Sweet Craving

Ginny Dyer

Creator of In Bloom Bakery

PAGE STREET
PUBLISHING CO.

PAGE STREET
PUBLISHING CO.

Copyright © 2022 Ginny Dyer

First published in 2022 by
Page Street Publishing Co.
27 Congress Street, Suite 1511
Salem, MA 01970
www.pagestreetpublishing.com

Distributed by Macmillan, sales in Canada by The Canadian Manda Group.

26 25 24 23 22   1 2 3 4 5

ISBN-13: 978-1-64567-641-6
ISBN-10: 1-64567-641-2

Library of Congress Control Number: 2022939216

Cover and book design by Page Street Publishing Co.
Photography by Ginny Dyer

Printed and bound in the United States of America

To Trisha, who put the love of baking in my heart from a young age, and to Kevin, who knew about this dream first.

Contents

Introduction

Welcome to *Petite, Pretty & Piped,* a deep dive into the world of cupcake and mini cake making that both novice and experienced bakers alike will find exciting! Here you will find recipes that are aesthetically pleasing and mouthwateringly delicious. Included are 40 cupcake and 20 mini cake recipes, each with a unique and exciting flavor concept.

Baking has always been my solace. From an early age, I was in the kitchen with my mom learning to bake; it was a happy place where I was free to explore and stretch my creative muscles. I believe it deeply affected how I developed as a person; it made me more imaginative, spontaneous and fun. I've always had a fascination with mixing different ingredients together and trying new things, and that is what I now get to do in my professional life with my baking blog, In Bloom Bakery.

I especially love baking cupcakes and cakes because there are so many different flavor concepts to experiment with. This book is my creative heart and soul poured out—all the exciting flavors I want the world to see in cupcake and mini cake form. Each base recipe features a similar, approachable foundation so you'll be able to refine your baking skills and achieve moist, delicious cakes every single time. But if you think this will make for boring bakes, think again! Each and every frosting, topping and filling has been thoughtfully developed to create a fun and unique flavor profile, so you'll never get tired of baking from this book!

My hope is that through this guide you will fall in love with baking mini desserts as much as I have. May it bring you joy and comfort and add carefree delight to your life. May it be an escape from the world around us, where we can relax our minds, be creative and forget about our worries, if even for just a moment.

I truly hope these recipes are ones that you and yours will adore for years to come. Thank you for being here and exploring in the kitchen with me. Let's begin this beautiful journey and get right down to making some petite and pretty mini cakes and cupcakes!

With love,

Important Ingredients

A mini cake or cupcake is only as good as its ingredients! Always use the highest-quality ingredients you can. Below, I expand on the most common ingredients you'll need to make these recipes and the purpose each one serves.

Baking Soda and Baking Powder: These two very important ingredients are what give cakes and cupcakes their perfect fluffy texture. Without these, baked goods would be super flat and unappealing. Baking soda is on average three times more potent than baking powder, so you'll see most recipes call for a teeny amount of baking soda instead of baking powder.

Butter: Ahh, my favorite ingredient. All the recipes in this book use butter instead of oil. Cakes made with butter tend to be softer and have a more tender texture than cakes made with oil. Butter also adds the best flavor to cakes that you really just can't replicate with oil. Butter is also used in almost all the frosting recipes in this book. For all recipes, unless otherwise indicated, use unsalted butter for the best results.

Buttermilk: Buttermilk is used in many recipes in this book. It adds extra moisture and reacts with the leavening agents to give the cakes and cupcakes the perfect rise. If you don't have buttermilk on hand, you can always make your own by mixing ½ tablespoon (7 ml) of fresh lemon juice or white vinegar with ½ cup (120 ml) of whole milk or half-and-half.

Cake Flour and All-Purpose Flour: Cake flour is super finely ground and has a very low protein content. Because of this, cakes baked with cake flour are much lighter, airier and have a looser crumb. Think of fluffy white cake. All-purpose flour has a higher protein content than cake flour. Cakes baked with all-purpose flour have a tighter crumb and more of a "bite" to them. Think of moist chocolate cake. Cake flour also weighs less per cup than all-purpose flour, so for best results, use the kind of flour each recipe specifies.

Chocolate: Four different kinds of chocolate are used in this book: milk, dark, white and ruby. I highly recommend using the highest quality chocolate bars you can, like Lindt® or Ghirardelli®. Doing so will give you the very best frostings and ganaches.

Cocoa Powder: The two kinds of cocoa powder used in this book are natural and Dutch process. Natural cocoa powder gives you that classic, mild chocolate taste, while Dutch process cocoa powder offers rich dark-chocolate notes. Each recipe will specify which to use, and results are best if the kind indicated is used.

Cream Cheese: Many of the recipes in this book are frosted with delicious, melt-in-your-mouth cream cheese frosting. I recommend using full-fat cream cheese, as it will give you a more stable consistency and overall better taste.

Eggs: Eggs add structure to cakes and cupcakes. Egg whites create light and airy cake, while yolks add extra moisture and produce a more rich and tender cake. In all the recipes in this book, minus the brownie cupcakes (page 121), eggs or egg whites are whipped into creamed butter and sugar, which adds air to the batter. This results in a perfect textured crumb, and cakes and cupcakes that rise beautifully. I recommend using large eggs for all the recipes in this book.

Salt: Salt accentuates all the flavors in cakes and cupcakes. Without it, baked goods would be extremely boring in taste. I recommend using sea salt for the best flavor.

Sugar: Granulated white sugar and light brown sugar are used in these cake and cupcake recipes to, of course, add sweetness but also moisture. Powdered sugar is used to sweeten the various frostings in this book.

Vanilla and Other Extracts: This book uses all sorts of extracts. Vanilla, orange, lemon, almond, lavender, peppermint, hazelnut, coconut and even butter extracts, to name a few, are used to add unique flavor to particular recipes. I love to use vanilla bean paste when I can, as it adds the best and most concentrated vanilla flavor.

Baking Tools

These are all the tools necessary for making the best mini cakes and cupcakes! They will help you make perfect frostings, the best cake batter and the prettiest piping.

4-inch (10-cm) Cake Pans: All the mini cake recipes will require three 4-inch (10-cm) cake pans. Heavy-duty aluminum cake pans will be your best option.

4-inch (10-cm) Parchment Paper Rounds: These help prevent the mini cakes from sticking to the bottoms of the pans.

Cake Scraper: This tool ensures your mini cake's frosting will be even. It allows you to easily scrape the frosting across the outside of the cake, leaving a smooth layer behind.

Cake Turntable: This is essential for frosting mini cakes. It makes it so much easier to get a pretty and even layer of frosting on the outside of the cake.

Cupcake Corer: This will help you prepare the filled cupcake recipes in this book. It easily removes the center of cupcakes, leaving a perfect hole to be filled with the various jams, ganaches, caramels and pastry creams.

Cupcake Liners: Liners are used to keep the cupcakes from sticking to the pan. For pretty and fun results, use different color liners for different recipes, like dark brown for cholate cupcakes or pink for the Champagne & Chambord Cupcakes (page 126).

Cupcake Pan: The cupcake recipes in this book will require a 12-cup cupcake pan. A heavy-duty aluminum cupcake pan is the best option.

Electric Stand Mixer: This will be your baking best friend. It allows you to whip up the various batters and frosting recipes in this book very easily. Use a paddle attachment for the batters and the whisk attachment for the frostings. (An electric hand mixer will also get the job done.)

Kitchen Scale: A digital kitchen scale allows you to measure ingredients precisely so that you're not over- or undermeasuring. You can also easily divide cake batter evenly between cake pans by weighing the batter in the pans. They're so helpful and I can't recommend them enough!

Large Cookie Scoop: This tool is super useful for easily scooping cupcake batter into the liners. A 2-tablespoon (30-ml) scoop works best.

Measuring Cups: If you choose to not go the digital kitchen scale route, you can get very similar measurements using measuring cups. Just be sure to spoon and level flour when indicated in recipes. (See the Tips for Making the Best Cake Batter on page 9, for more on this.) Use a liquid measuring cup for things like buttermilk and milk and opt for a dry measuring cup for things like molasses, sour cream, caramel and, of course, flour and sugar.

Measuring Spoons: Ingredients like extracts and leavening agents that are too small to weigh require measuring spoons. Because all the recipes in this book are for mini creations, many measurements are very small. You will need an ⅛ teaspoon measuring spoon for almost all the recipes in this book. Having a specific ¾ teaspoon measuring spoon will also come in handy.

Mini Offset Spatula: You will surely need a mini offset spatula to efficiently assemble your mini cakes. The design of an offset spatula allows you to easily spread frosting evenly on your cake layers.

Piping Bags: I love to use disposable piping bags, as it makes life so much easier. These are used to fill the cupcakes with jams, ganaches and pastry creams, pipe cupcakes with frosting and add drips to mini cakes.

Piping Tips: The various tips used in this book are Wilton® 1M, 2D and 8B, but feel free to use any other tips you love!

Sifter: This handy tool is vital for removing lumps from your flours and powdered sugar. For the recipes in this book, measure your flour or powdered sugar, then sift it.

Small Bowls: The recipes in this book are mini so you'll be working with very small portions of things like ganache. Having small bowls on hand will make executing these recipes much easier.

Small Wooden Sticks: Mini cakes can be difficult to assemble and stand up straight. I recommend using wooden sticks or drinking straws to reinforce the cake, so it doesn't lean.

Spatulas: You can't really bake a cake without spatulas! I love silicone spatulas for easily scraping down the sides of the bowl when making cake batter or frosting. Mini spatulas are also very helpful when making the various fillings and ganaches for these recipes.

Tips for Making the Best Cake Batter

All the cake and cupcake batters in this book are very similar. My hope is that the more recipes you make, the more you'll understand how the batters should look at each step. It's my intention that the recipes are as straightforward and easy to follow as possible, but in case you're having difficulty, please read through this section for tips on how to perfect your batters. I also include storage and make-ahead tips here.

Measure Flour Properly

To ensure your cakes and cupcakes come out perfectly each time, it is essential that you measure your ingredients properly, especially your flour. I cannot recommend a digital kitchen scale enough. Every baker should own one, as they ensure that your measurements are always exactly precise. All the recipes in this book have been meticulously tested and offer both standard US measurements and metric measurements. If you do not wish to use a kitchen scale, please follow the "spooned and leveled" method for measuring flour so that each recipe uses just the right amount of flour. To do this, sprinkle spoonfuls of flour into your measuring cup and swipe the excess off with the back of a knife. Be careful not to pack in the flour, and never scoop a measuring cup directly into your flour. I do note in some areas of the book to scoop and level things like cornstarch and cocoa powder because this gives you more exact measurements, similar to weighing the ingredients.

Wet Ingredient Tips

When making your cake batters, be sure that all your wet ingredients are at room temperature. Butter should be soft. Buttermilk, eggs, sour cream and milk should be room temperature to the touch. It is important that wet ingredients are room temperature rather than cold because cold wet ingredients lead to a dense and sometimes gummy cake consistency. Room temperature wet ingredients will yield a more soft and tender cake.

Mixing Tips

Be careful not to overmix your batters. Mixing for longer than a recipe calls for causes more air to be added to the batter. This can lead to the recipe yielding what seems like too much batter. In the instance of cupcake recipes, this can mean that you'll have more batter than for just 12 cupcake wells. If you try to fit it all into the cupcake wells, you'll end up with overfilled cupcake liners, which will cause the batter to spill over when it's baking. Mix the batters for as long and at the speed that the recipe says. To yield the very best results, I recommend using the paddle attachment of a stand mixer for making all the cupcake and cake batters in this book.

Making Mini Cakes and Cupcakes Ahead of Time

While I always recommend baking cakes or cupcakes fresh for the best taste, I understand sometimes you want to make things ahead. If choosing this option, bake the cake or cupcakes as usual and let them cool completely. *For mini cakes,* wrap each layer in plastic wrap and place them in an airtight container or baggie. *For cupcakes,* place the cupcakes in an airtight container or baggie. Freeze the wrapped cake layers or cupcakes for up to a week. Let them defrost completely before attempting to assemble the mini cake or cupcakes.

Tips for Making Perfect Frosting

The frosting recipes in this book are a mixture of different buttercreams and cream cheese frostings. Most of the frosting recipes are made in similar ways and should be increasingly easier to make the more recipes you try. This section will help you troubleshoot as well as give helpful tips on how to make the best frostings.

Tips on Butter

Decorating cakes and cupcakes can be a tricky skill to master, and a huge determining factor for how your cake will turn out is the consistency of your frosting. Buttercreams tend to be more stable, and cream cheese frostings are softer. For the best results with each, when you're ready to decorate, make sure your butter is softened but not so soft that it can't hold its form. I find that about an hour out of the fridge is usually the perfect consistency.

Tips on Whipping

The start of a good buttercream or cream cheese frosting is how well the butter is whipped. Be sure to whip your butter until it is extremely pale, almost white, and very fluffy. It should be almost unrecognizable and doubled in size from what you started with. It does take some patience, as it can sometimes take up to 10 minutes to get it to the perfect consistency.

After the powdered sugar has been incorporated, be sure to keep whipping the frosting on high speed for at least 1 more minute, until it is light and fluffy. A good frosting is all in how much it is whipped. I recommend using the whisk attachment of a stand mixer for making all the frosting recipes in this book.

Tips on Cream Cheese

When making cream cheese frosting, be sure your cream cheese is cold, right from the fridge. This makes the frosting more stable than if the cream cheese were to be softened to room temperature. Add the cream cheese to the very whipped butter and mix on medium-high speed for 1 to 2 minutes, until thoroughly combined with no lumps, *then* sift in the powdered sugar. Making sure the cream cheese is properly mixed into the butter before adding in powdered sugar will give you perfectly smooth and creamy cream cheese frosting.

Troubleshooting Droopy Frosting

If your frosting gets too warm and starts to droop on you, place your mixing bowl with the frosting in the fridge for 5 to 10 minutes to allow it to firm up. Then whip it again until it's fluffy. This should help you to have the perfect consistency at all times. When decorating cakes, it is a good idea to re-whip the frosting between applications of frosting the layers.

A Note on Frosting Sweetness

All frosting recipes in this book have been sweetened to match their cake and cupcake counterpart of the recipe. That being said, feel free to add powdered sugar to your sweetness preference. Do note, however, that adding less powdered sugar will change the frosting's consistency. It can result in an unstable frosting that makes it difficult to decorate the mini cakes.

Tips on Making Chocolate Frosting

Most frosting recipes in the Chocolate Cravings chapter (page 17), and some recipes elsewhere, use melted chocolate of some kind. To ensure your frosting comes out great, make sure that the chocolate is melted and then allowed to cool slightly so that it does not melt the butter. If you wait until it is too cooled, it can harden once it's added to the butter. You'll want it to be completely liquid, but just about room temperature. This will result in perfect frosting every time!

Tips on Making Frosting with Alcohol

Because the frosting recipes in the Cocktails & Cordials chapter (page 125) include alcohol, they tend to be very "soft." I recommend putting the prepared frosting in the fridge for 10 to 15 minutes to help it firm up before using it on the mini cakes and cupcakes. You may have to do this a few times while assembling the mini cakes.

Making Frosting Ahead of Time

If you would prefer to make the frosting ahead of time before using it on the mini cakes and cupcakes, prepare the frosting as usual and then transfer it to a baggie or storage container. Refrigerate the frosting for 3 to 4 days or freeze it for up to 1 week. When ready to use, let the frosting come to near room temperature, then re-whip it until it is back to its original consistency.

Assembling and Storing Mini Cakes

This section is intended to be a guide on how to assemble the mini cakes in this book. You'll want to account 1½ to 2 hours to assemble the mini cakes from start to finish. Make sure you have your cake turntable, offset spatula, piping bags, piping tips, wooden sticks and cake scraper handy. Let's get down to business!

Step 1

To ensure the cake layers stack properly, the cake tops will most likely need to be evened out, as most dome while baking. With a sharp knife cut off each cake top so that every layer is even. Add a dollop of frosting to the bottom of the cake turntable.

Step 2

For mini cakes that just use just frosting, follow these steps. Place the first cake layer on the cake turntable. Then add a generous amount of frosting on top of the cake layer and even it out with your offset spatula, turning the cake turntable as you go. Place the next layer over top and repeat the step.

For mini cakes that use filling and frosting, follow these steps. See photos below and on page 13. Place the first cake layer on the cake turntable. Then add a thin layer of frosting on top of the cake layer and even it out with your offset spatula, turning the cake turntable as you go. Add some of the frosting to a piping bag fitted with a circular tip or cut some of the tip off of the piping bag. With the piping bag of frosting, pipe a "border" layer of frosting just on the edges of the cake layer. Make sure the border of frosting is about ¼ inch (6 mm) thick and about ½ inch (1.3 cm) high. Then add about one-third of the filling onto the cake layer. Place the next cake layer over top and repeat the step.

Mini Cakes That Use Filling & Frosting

Blueberry Cobbler Mini Cake (page 61)

Roasted Strawberries & Cream Mini Cake (page 79)

Lemon Basil Blueberry Jam Mini Cake (page 88)

Salted Caramel Apple Mini Cake (page 157)

Thin layer of frosting on cake layer

Border of frosting with filling in the middle

Step 3

Place the final cake layer over the top. At this point, consider inserting three to four wooden sticks or plastic straws through the top of the cake to reinforce it so that it won't lean. (Cut the straws to fit the cake's height.) Then place small dollops of frosting on the outer edges and top of the cake. Even out the frosting as much as possible with your offset spatula.

Step 4

With your cake scraper, scrape the icing across the cake, turning the cake turntable as you go to make the process as easy as possible. This layer of frosting should be very thin. This is called the "crumb layer" and will ensure that the cake's final coating of frosting is smooth and free of crumbs. Once the crumb layer of frosting has been applied, refrigerate the cake for at least 30 minutes to allow the frosting to firm up. (Some mini cake recipes in this book were decorated in a naked fashion. All recipes will make enough frosting to coat the entire cake; however, if you want to leave some naked, the crumb coat also serves as that naked look.)

Step 5

Once the cake has chilled in the fridge, remove it and apply the final coating of frosting. You may need to re-whip the frosting by mixing it on high for 1 minute or so. Apply generous dollops of frosting on the sides and top of the cake and smooth them out with your offset spatula. With your cake scraper, even out the frosting, turning the cake turntable as you go. Chill the cake for 20 to 25 minutes if it will have a ganache or caramel drip. This will allow the drip to set better as it runs down the sides of the cake.

Crumb coat

Final frosting layer

Step 6

If the mini cake recipe calls for a ganache or caramel drip, follow these steps. Transfer the ganache to a piping bag and cut a small hole in the bottom of it. Go around the top edges of the cake and squeeze the ganache so it starts to drip down the sides of the cake. A good tip is to space out your drips about every quarter- to half-inch (6-mm to 1-cm). Also, squeeze ganache around the top of the cake and smooth it out slightly with a clean offset spatula. As the ganache sits it will smooth out and come together to form a beautiful finish on top of the cake. Place the cake back in the fridge for at least 30 minutes to allow the ganache or caramel to set. (An exception to this final chilling is the Almond Amaretto Mini Cake [page 133]. Its caramel is thinner and won't really set; it should be served right after applying the drip.)

Note: If the caramel or ganache gets too firm, rewarm it for 10 to 15 seconds in the microwave or 1 to 2 minutes in a small saucepan over low heat to make it easier to work with. Then proceed using it for the drip. You'll want each to be near room temperature. When at the correct temperature, the ganache should easily drip from the piping bag without being super runny, and the caramel should form firm drips.

Mini Cakes with a Drip

Caramelized White Chocolate Mini Cake (page 21)

Milk Chocolate Peanut Butter Banana Mini Cake (page 27)

Milk Chocolate Malt Mini Cake (page 33)

Dulce de Leche Churro Mini Cake (page 53)

Boston Cream Pie Mini Cake (page 69)

Salted Caramel Banana Bread Mini Cake (page 91)

Salted Caramel Latte Mini Cake (page 100)

Chocolate Chip Cookie Dough Mini Cake (page 109)

Ruby Chocolate Mini Cake (page 122)

White Russian Mini Cake (page 130)

Almond Amaretto Mini Cake (page 133)

Hazelnut Frangelico® Mini Cake (page 147)

Pumpkin Butterscotch Mini Cake (page 150)

Salted Caramel Apple Mini Cake (page 157)

If the mini cake recipe uses filling on top of the cake, follow these steps. Spoon the remaining filling over the top of the cake. See the recipe photos to see whether the filling should drip down the cake and how else to decorate it.

Mini Cakes with Filling on Top

Blueberry Cobbler Mini Cake (page 61)

Roasted Strawberries & Cream Mini Cake (page 79)

Lemon Basil Blueberry Jam Mini Cake (page 88)

For cakes that are decorated with swirls of frosting, follow these steps. Re-whip the remaining frosting, if need be, then transfer it to a piping bag fitted with a decorative tip. Pipe decorative swirls of frosting on top of the cake, then decorate the mini cake however else you see fit. See the recipe photos for decoration ideas. Then the cake is ready to serve!

Storing Leftover Mini Cakes

Store leftover mini cakes in an airtight container in the fridge for up to 3 days. Most mini cakes will taste best at room temperature. Take them out of the fridge about 30 minutes before enjoying. You can also freeze leftovers for up to a week. Just ensure that leftover mini cakes are in an airtight container, and even consider wrapping individual slices in plastic wrap before putting them in a storage container to freeze.

Assembling and Storing Filled Cupcakes

This section's purpose is to be a guide on assembling the filled cupcakes in this book. The process for cupcakes is more straightforward than it is for assembling mini cakes, but I wanted to make sure we covered it all! Have your cupcake corer, piping bags and piping tips ready. Let's fill some cupcakes!

Step 1
Once the cupcakes are completely cooled, remove a bit of the centers of each cupcake. A cupcake corer really comes in handy for this. It will remove the centers with little effort. You can also use a small spoon or knife for this step if you don't have a cupcake corer.

Step 2
Add your cupcake's filling to a piping bag fitted with a circular tip, then cut off the tip of the bag. Pipe ganache, jam or whatever other filling you're using into the center of each cupcake. Some cupcake recipes will use filling that is too thick to be piped in, like the Bourbon Pecan Pie Cupcakes (page 153), Everything but the Kitchen Sink Cupcakes (page 115) and Magic Cookie Bar Cupcakes (page 117), for example. In these cases, use a small spoon to add the filling to each cupcake.

Step 3
Add the frosting to a piping bag fitted with your favorite decorative tip. Pipe a generous amount of frosting onto each cupcake. I always like to start with one swirl as the base and build an additional swirl on top for more height.

Step 4
My favorite part—decorate your cupcakes! See the recipe photos for decorating ideas, or embellish them however you see fit. Then serve!

Storing Leftover Cupcakes
Store leftover cupcakes in an airtight container in the fridge for up to 3 days. Most cupcakes will taste best at room temperature. Take them out of the fridge about 30 minutes before enjoying. You can also freeze leftovers for up to a week. Just ensure that leftover cupcakes are in an airtight container, and even consider wrapping individual cupcakes in plastic wrap before putting them in a storage container to freeze.

Cored

Filled

Frosted

Chocolate Cravings

"Chocolate is forever"—that's how the saying goes, doesn't it? Chocolate holds a special place in all our hearts and thus deserves center stage as the first chapter in this book. Whether you're partial to dark, milk or white chocolate, you'll find that every flavor has its place in this chapter. In this section, you'll find unique chocolate flavor pairings in the form of Caramelized White Chocolate Mini Cake (page 21), Dark Chocolate Cherry Cabernet Cupcakes (page 37), Milk Chocolate Peanut Butter Banana Mini Cake (page 27) and Dark Chocolate Mint Cupcakes (page 41). Chocolate lovers are sure to adore these decadent chocolate creations.

Most frosting recipes in this chapter use melted chocolate of some kind. To ensure your frosting turns out great, make sure that the chocolate is melted and then allowed to cool slightly so that it does not melt the butter. If you wait until it is too cooled, it can harden once it's added to the butter. You'll want it to be completely liquid, but nearly room temperature. Following this advice will result in perfect frosting every time!

Dark Chocolate Peanut Butter Cup Cupcakes

Name a better dessert combination than chocolate and peanut butter . . . I'll wait! These dark chocolate cupcakes are filled with an out-of-this-world peanut butter chip ganache and topped with a piping of smooth peanut butter buttercream. The combination of chocolate and peanut butter always seems to be everyone's favorite, and these cupcakes are sure to wow every peanut butter cup fan you know.

Yield: 12 cupcakes

For the Dark Chocolate Cupcakes

1 cup (125 g) all-purpose flour, spooned and leveled

5 tbsp (25 g) Dutch process cocoa powder, scooped and leveled

½ tsp baking powder

½ tsp baking soda

¼ tsp salt

1 tsp espresso powder (optional)

¼ cup (56 g) unsalted butter, softened

¾ cup (150 g) granulated sugar

1 egg, at room temperature

1 egg yolk, at room temperature

1 tsp vanilla bean paste or extract

½ cup (120 ml) milk, at room temperature

¼ cup (61 g) sour cream, at room temperature

For the Peanut Butter Chip Ganache

5 tbsp (75 ml) heavy cream

½ cup (100 g) peanut butter chips (I prefer Reese's® brand)

For the Peanut Butter Buttercream

¾ cup (168 g) unsalted butter, softened

⅛ tsp salt

6 tbsp (96 g) peanut butter (see Note)

1½ cups (195 g) powdered sugar

½ tsp vanilla bean paste or extract

6 peanut butter cups, halved for decoration (optional)

To make the dark chocolate cupcakes, preheat the oven to 350°F (177°C). Line a cupcake pan with 12 liners and set aside. In a small bowl, sift together the flour, cocoa powder, baking powder, baking soda, salt and espresso powder (if using), then set aside. In a large bowl, cream the butter and sugar together with an electric mixer on high speed for 2 to 3 minutes, until fluffy. Then add the egg, egg yolk and vanilla and mix on medium-high speed for 1 to 2 minutes, or until the mixture is pale, smooth and slightly fluffy. Scrape the sides and bottom of the bowl with a spatula as necessary.

Add the milk and sour cream and mix on medium speed until combined. The mixture will look curdled at this point, but don't worry. Add the dry ingredients to the wet ingredients a little at a time, until all has been added, mixing on low, then medium, speed for each addition. Mix just until the batter is combined and smooth, scraping the sides and bottom of the bowl as necessary. The batter will be a little thin.

(continued)

Divide the batter evenly among the 12 liners until each is about three-quarters full. Bake the cupcakes for 16 to 19 minutes, or until a cake tester or toothpick comes out clean from the centers. Let the cupcakes cool in the pan for 10 minutes, then transfer them to a cooling rack to finish cooling.

Work on the peanut butter chip ganache while the cupcakes are baking. Add the heavy cream to a medium-sized bowl and microwave it for 35 to 45 seconds or heat it over the stove in a small saucepan just until steaming, then transfer it to a medium bowl. Add the peanut butter chips and stir to combine. Let the ganache cool completely, stirring so that it cools evenly. It will thicken as it cools. Once cooled, whip the ganache on high speed with an electric mixer for about 1 minute, until it is pale and fluffy. Transfer the ganache to a piping bag and cut off the tip when ready to use.

To make the peanut butter buttercream, add the butter and salt to a large bowl. With an electric mixer at high speed, whip until the butter is pale, fluffy and doubled in size. This should take 5 to 10 minutes. Then add the peanut butter and mix on medium speed until combined. Next, sift the powdered sugar into the mixture ½ cup (65 g) at a time. Mix on low, then medium, speed, making sure each addition is fully combined before adding the next. Scrape the sides and bottom of the bowl as necessary. When the last addition has been combined, add the vanilla and mix on high speed for about 1 minute, until the frosting is light and fluffy. Transfer the frosting to a piping bag fitted with a decorative tip.

Please see page 15 for cupcake assembly instructions, and use the peanut butter chip ganache and peanut butter buttercream when indicated. Garnish with mini peanut butter cups (if using), then serve!

Note: Use Jif® or a similar kind of peanut butter and not natural peanut butter. Natural peanut butter has too much peanut oil in it and can cause the frosting to split.

Caramelized White Chocolate Mini Cake

Caramelized white chocolate is truly the cat's meow. I like to think of it like regular white chocolate's fancy cousin. For this mini cake, silky smooth white chocolate gets baked at a low temperature until it is caramelized to golden-brown perfection. It's then used to make the delicious buttercream frosting and ganache drip, which envelop a moist and perfectly tender brown sugar vanilla cake. White chocolate fans beware: This one is truly addicting.

Yield: 1 (4-inch [10-cm]) three-tier cake

For the Caramelized White Chocolate
6 oz (170 g) high-quality white chocolate, chopped (Lindt was used)

For the Cake
1 cup + 2 tbsp (141 g) all-purpose flour, spooned and leveled

¾ tsp baking powder

⅛ tsp baking soda

¼ tsp salt

5 tbsp (70 g) unsalted butter, softened

½ cup (100 g) granulated sugar

¼ cup (55 g) light brown sugar, packed

1 egg, at room temperature

1 egg yolk, at room temperature

1 tsp vanilla bean paste or extract

½ cup (120 ml) buttermilk, at room temperature

For the Caramelized White Chocolate Buttercream
¾ cup (168 g) unsalted butter, softened

⅛ tsp salt

3 oz (85 g) caramelized white chocolate, melted and slightly cooled

1½ cups (195 g) powdered sugar

For the Caramelized White Chocolate Ganache Drip
1 tbsp (15 ml) heavy cream

1½ oz (42 g) caramelized white chocolate, chopped, plus more for decorating

Make the caramelized white chocolate first. Preheat the oven to 250°F (121°C). Sprinkle the chopped white chocolate over a baking sheet. Bake the chocolate for 1 hour and 20 minutes, stirring the chocolate every 10 minutes with a silicone spatula. Make sure to flatten it as best as you can each time. At first the chocolate will look dry and chalky, but as it continues to bake it will get smooth and glossy like regular melted chocolate. When the baking time is up, smooth out the chocolate and let it cool completely in the fridge. Once it is completely cooled, the caramelized white chocolate will be easy to remove from the baking sheet. Remove it and then chop in small pieces to use in the rest of the recipe.

To make the cake, preheat the oven to 350°F (177°C). Spray three 4-inch (10-cm) cake pans with nonstick spray. In a small bowl, sift together the all-purpose flour, baking powder, baking soda and salt, then set aside. In a large bowl, cream the butter, granulated sugar and brown sugar together with an electric mixer on high for 2 to 3 minutes, until fluffy. Then add the egg, egg yolk and vanilla and mix on medium-high for 1 to 2 minutes, or until the mixture is pale and smooth. Scrape the sides and bottom of the bowl with a spatula as necessary.

(continued)

Add the dry ingredients and the buttermilk to the butter mixture a little at a time until all has been added, mixing on low, then medium, speed for each addition. Mix just until the batter is combined and smooth, scraping the sides of the bowl as necessary.

Divide the batter evenly among the cake pans. Bake the cakes for 26 to 30 minutes, or until a cake tester or toothpick comes out clean from the centers. Let the cakes cool in their pans for 2 minutes, then transfer them to a cooling rack to finish cooling.

Make the caramelized white chocolate buttercream while waiting for the cakes to cool. Add the butter and salt to a large bowl. Whip with an electric mixer on high speed for 5 to 10 minutes until the butter is pale, fluffy and doubled in size. Pour in the melted and slightly cooled caramelized white chocolate and combine on medium speed. Then sift the powdered sugar into the mixture ½ cup (65 g) at a time. Mix on low, then medium, speed, making sure each addition is fully combined before adding the next. Scrape the sides of the bowl as necessary. After the last of the powdered sugar has been added, mix on high speed for about 1 minute, until the frosting is light and fluffy.

To make the caramelized white chocolate ganache, add the heavy cream to a small bowl and microwave for 20 to 25 seconds or heat it over the stove in a small saucepan until steaming, then transfer it to a small bowl. Add the chopped caramelized white chocolate and stir to combine. Let the ganache cool slightly and then transfer it to a piping bag. The ganache should be slightly warm but not hot when ready to use on the cake.

Please see page 12 for mini cake assembly instructions, using the caramelized white chocolate buttercream and caramelized white chocolate ganache when indicated. Decorate with extra caramelized white chocolate, then serve!

German Chocolate Cupcakes

They call them classics for a reason! Sometimes all you need is just a good, timeless dessert and these German chocolate cupcakes definitely deliver. These tender chocolate cupcakes are frosted with a silky milk chocolate buttercream and finished with a scoop of luscious coconut pecan topping. Each bite of moist chocolate cupcake and gooey topping will remind you why German chocolate cake is a tried-and-true classic.

Yield: 12 cupcakes

For the Coconut Pecan Topping

½ cup (110 g) brown sugar

1 egg yolk

2 tbsp (28 g) unsalted butter

½ tsp vanilla bean paste or extract

½ cup (120 ml) evaporated milk

⅛ tsp salt

¾ cup (68 g) sweetened shredded coconut

¼ cup (27 g) chopped pecans

For the Chocolate Cupcakes

1 cup (125 g) all-purpose flour, spooned and leveled

5 tbsp (25 g) natural cocoa powder, scooped and leveled

½ tsp baking powder

½ tsp baking soda

¼ tsp salt

½ tsp espresso powder (optional)

¼ cup (56 g) unsalted butter, softened

¾ cup (150 g) granulated sugar

1 egg, at room temperature

1 egg yolk, at room temperature

1 tsp vanilla bean paste or extract

½ cup (120 ml) milk, at room temperature

¼ cup (61 g) sour cream, at room temperature

For the Milk Chocolate Buttercream

¾ cup (168 g) unsalted butter, softened

⅛ tsp salt

3 oz (85 g) milk chocolate, melted and slightly cooled

5 tbsp (25 g) natural cocoa powder, scooped and leveled

1½ cups (195 g) powdered sugar

1-2 tbsp (15–30 ml) heavy cream

Make the coconut pecan topping first so it has plenty of time to cool. Add the brown sugar, egg yolk, butter, vanilla, evaporated milk and salt to a medium-sized saucepan. Stir to combine. Heat for about 10 minutes over medium-low heat, stirring frequently, until thick and smooth. Remove from the heat and mix in the coconut and pecans. Let the mixture cool completely before using it on the cupcakes.

To make the chocolate cupcakes, preheat the oven to 350°F (177°C). Line a cupcake pan with 12 liners and set aside. In a small bowl, sift together the flour, cocoa powder, baking powder, baking soda, salt and espresso powder (if using), then set aside. In a large bowl, cream the butter and sugar together with an electric mixer on high speed for 2 to 3 minutes, until fluffy. Then add the egg, egg yolk and vanilla and mix on medium-high speed for 1 to 2 minutes, or until the mixture is pale, smooth and slightly fluffy. Scrape the sides and bottom of the bowl with a spatula as necessary.

(continued)

Next, add the milk and sour cream and mix on medium speed until combined. The mixture will look curdled at this point, but don't worry. Add the dry ingredients to the wet ingredients a little at a time until all has been added, mixing on low, then medium, speed for each addition. Mix just until the batter is combined and smooth, scraping the sides of the bowl as necessary. The batter will be a little thin.

Divide the batter evenly among the 12 liners until each is about three-quarters full. Bake the cupcakes for 16 to 19 minutes, or until a cake tester or toothpick comes out clean from the centers. Let the cupcakes cool in the pan for 10 minutes, then transfer them to a cooling rack to finish cooling.

Make the milk chocolate buttercream while waiting for the cupcakes to cool. In a large bowl, combine the butter and salt. Whip with an electric mixer on high speed for 5 to 10 minutes, until the butter is pale, fluffy and doubled in size. Pour in the melted and slightly cooled milk chocolate and combine on medium speed. Then sift in the cocoa powder and mix on low, then medium, speed until combined. Next, sift the powdered sugar into the mixture ½ cup (65 g) at a time.

Mix on low, then medium, speed, making sure each addition is fully combined before adding the next. Scrape the sides of the bowl as necessary. After the last of the powdered sugar has been added, pour in the heavy cream and mix on high speed for about 1 minute, until the frosting is light and fluffy. Transfer the frosting to a piping bag fitted with a decorative tip.

When the cupcakes are cooled, pipe a "nest" of milk chocolate buttercream on top of each cupcake. Place about 1 tablespoon (15 g) of coconut pecan filling on top, then serve!

Milk Chocolate Peanut Butter Banana Mini Cake

Quite possibly the most tender cake you'll ever bake, this tiny creation packs in all the flavor combinations you never knew you needed in your life. A decadent, soft chocolate banana cake is filled and frosted with silky milk chocolate peanut butter buttercream. The cake boasts a beautiful peanut butter ganache drip and pretty swirls of decorative frosting. Peanut butter and chocolate fans alike will love the addition of banana to this classic flavor pairing.

Yield: 1 (4-inch [10-cm]) three-tier cake

For the Milk Chocolate Banana Cake
1 cup (125 g) all-purpose flour

5 tbsp (25 g) cocoa powder, scooped and leveled

½ tsp baking powder

½ tsp baking soda

¼ tsp salt

¼ cup (56 g) unsalted butter, softened

¾ cup (150 g) granulated sugar

1 egg, at room temperature

1 egg yolk, at room temperature

1 tsp vanilla bean paste or extract

½ cup (125 g) mashed banana

¼ cup (60 ml) whole milk, at room temperature

For the Milk Chocolate Peanut Butter Buttercream Frosting
¾ cup (168 g) unsalted butter, softened

⅛ tsp salt

¼ cup (64 g) creamy peanut butter (see Note)

2 oz (56 g) milk chocolate, melted and slightly cooled

¼ cup (20 g) cocoa powder

1½ cups (195 g) powdered sugar

½–1 tbsp (7–15 ml) heavy cream

For the Peanut Butter Ganache Drip
2 tbsp (30 ml) heavy cream

1½ oz (42 g) peanut butter chips

Chopped peanuts, for decoration (optional)

Banana slices, for decoration (optional)

Milk chocolate pieces, for decoration (optional)

To make the milk chocolate banana cake, preheat the oven to 350°F (177°C). Spray three 4-inch (10-cm) cake pans with nonstick spray. In a small bowl, sift the all-purpose flour, cocoa powder, baking powder, baking soda and salt, then set aside. In a large bowl, cream the butter and granulated sugar together with an electric mixer on high speed for 2 to 3 minutes, until fluffy. Add the egg, egg yolk and vanilla and mix on medium-high for 1 to 2 minutes, or until the mixture is pale, smooth and slightly fluffy. Scrape the sides and bottom of the bowl with a spatula as necessary.

Add the mashed banana and mix on medium speed just until combined. Alternate adding the dry ingredients and the milk to the butter mixture a little at a time until each has been completely incorporated. Mix on low, then medium, speed for each addition. Mix until the batter is combined and smooth, scraping the sides of the bowl as necessary.

(continued)

Divide the batter evenly among the cake pans. Bake the cakes for 25 to 29 minutes, or until a cake tester or toothpick comes out clean from the centers. Let the cakes cool in their pans for 2 minutes, then transfer them to a cooling rack to finish cooling.

Make the milk chocolate peanut butter buttercream while the cakes cool by adding the butter and salt to a large bowl. Whip with an electric mixer on high for 5 to 10 minutes, until the butter is pale, fluffy and doubled in size. Add the peanut butter and mix on medium speed until combined. Pour in the melted and slightly cooled milk chocolate and combine on medium speed. Then sift in the cocoa powder and mix on low, then medium, speed until combined. Next, sift the powdered sugar into the mixture ½ cup (65 g) at a time.

Mix on low, then medium, speed, making sure each addition is fully combined before adding the next. Scrape the sides of the bowl as necessary. When the last addition is added, pour in the heavy cream and mix on high speed for about 1 minute, until the frosting is light and fluffy.

To make the peanut butter ganache, add the heavy cream to a small bowl and microwave for 30 to 35 seconds, or heat it over the stove in a very small saucepan until steaming, then transfer to a small bowl. Add the peanut butter chips and stir to combine. Let the ganache cool slightly before using it on the cake. It should be warm but not hot.

Please see page 12 for mini cake assembly instructions, using the milk chocolate peanut butter buttercream and peanut butter ganache when indicated. Decorate with chopped peanuts, banana slices and milk chocolate pieces (if using), then serve and enjoy!

Note: Use Jif or a similar kind of peanut butter and not natural peanut butter. Natural peanut butter has too much peanut oil in it and can cause the frosting to split.

Triple Dark Chocolate Cupcakes

To me, nothing says decadence more than dark chocolate. To bring ultimate indulgence, I present these cupcakes with dark chocolate three ways. Moist dark chocolate cupcakes are filled with thick and dreamy dark chocolate ganache and topped with a generous piping of beautifully smooth dark chocolate buttercream frosting. These are sure to be a dream dessert for any chocolate lovers out there!

Yield: 12 cupcakes

For the Dark Chocolate Cupcakes
1 cup (125 g) all-purpose flour

5 tbsp (25 g) Dutch process cocoa powder, scooped and leveled

½ tsp baking powder

½ tsp baking soda

¼ tsp salt

1 tsp espresso powder (optional)

¼ cup (56 g) unsalted butter, softened

¾ cup (150 g) granulated sugar

1 egg, at room temperature

1 egg yolk, at room temperature

1 tsp vanilla bean paste or extract

½ cup (120 ml) milk, at room temperature

¼ cup (61 g) sour cream, at room temperature

For the Dark Chocolate Ganache
4 oz (113 g) dark chocolate, chopped

½ cup (120 ml) heavy cream

For the Dark Chocolate Buttercream
¾ cup (168 g) unsalted butter, softened

⅛ tsp salt

3 oz (85 g) dark chocolate, melted and slightly cooled

5 tbsp (25 g) Dutch process cocoa powder

1½ cups (195 g) powdered sugar

2–3 tbsp (30–45 ml) heavy cream

12 dark chocolate pieces, for decoration (optional)

Dark chocolate shavings, for decoration (optional)

To make the dark chocolate cupcakes, preheat the oven to 350°F (177°C). Line a cupcake pan with 12 liners and set aside. In a small bowl, sift together the flour, cocoa powder, baking powder, baking soda, salt and espresso powder (if using), then set aside. In a large bowl, cream the butter and sugar together with an electric mixer on high speed for 2 to 3 minutes, until fluffy. Add the egg, egg yolk and vanilla and mix on medium-high speed for 1 to 2 minutes, or until the mixture is pale, smooth and slightly fluffy. Scrape the sides and bottom of the bowl with a spatula as necessary. Next, add the milk and sour cream and mix on medium speed until combined. The mixture will look curdled at this point, but don't worry.

Add the dry ingredients to the wet ingredients a little at a time until all has been added, mixing on low, then medium, speed for each addition. Mix just until the batter is combined and smooth, scraping the sides and bottom of the bowl with a spatula as necessary. The batter will be a little thin.

Divide the batter evenly among the 12 liners until each is about three-quarters full. Bake the cupcakes for 16 to 19 minutes, or until a cake tester or toothpick comes out clean from the centers. Let the cupcakes cool in the pan for 10 minutes, then transfer them to a cooling rack to finish cooling.

(continued)

Make the dark chocolate ganache while the cupcakes bake. Add the chopped dark chocolate to a medium-sized bowl. Heat the cream in a small saucepan just until it's steaming or microwave it for about 45 seconds. Pour the cream over the chocolate. Let the chocolate stand for 1 minute, then mix to combine the cream and melted chocolate together. Let the ganache cool until thicker and just about room temperature. Stir it while it cools to ensure it does so evenly. Once the ganache is cooled, transfer it to a piping bag and cut a bit of the tip off when you're ready to use it.

Make the dark chocolate buttercream while waiting for the cupcakes to cool. In a large bowl, add the butter and salt. Whip with an electric mixer on high speed for 5 to 10 minutes, until the butter is pale, fluffy and doubled in size. Pour in the melted and slightly cooled dark chocolate and mix on medium speed until combined. Then sift in the cocoa powder and mix on low, then medium, speed until combined. Sift the powdered sugar into the mixture ½ cup (65 g) at a time.

Mix on low, then medium, speed, making sure each addition is fully combined before adding the next. Scrape the sides and bottom of the bowl as necessary. When the last addition is added, pour in the heavy cream and mix on high speed for about 1 minute, until the frosting is light and fluffy.

Please see page 15 for filled cupcake assembly instructions, and use the dark chocolate ganache and dark chocolate buttercream when indicated. Decorate with dark chocolate pieces and dark chocolate shavings (if using), then serve and enjoy!

Note: For best results, use Dutch process cocoa powder and dark chocolate that is 60% cocoa.

Milk Chocolate Malt Mini Cake

Nope, it's not a milkshake—it's a cake! Malt and milk chocolate just go so well together, and especially in mini cake form. Three layers of moist chocolate malt cake are frosted with the best milk chocolate malt buttercream that will truly make you feel like you're sipping a chocolate malt milkshake at an ice cream parlor. It's topped with a pretty milk chocolate ganache drip and chocolate malt balls for show. All my malt fans out there will adore this cake. This recipe is lovingly dedicated to Bill, Christian and Peyton. You and your obsessions with malt inspired this cake.

Yield: 1 (4-inch [10-cm]) three-tier cake

For the Chocolate Malt Cake

1 cup (125 g) all-purpose flour, spooned and leveled

5 tbsp (25 g) cocoa powder, scooped and leveled

¾ tsp baking powder

⅛ tsp baking soda

¼ tsp salt

½ tsp espresso powder (optional)

½ cup (120 ml) milk, at room temperature

6 tbsp (48 g) malted milk powder, spooned and leveled; Nestle® was used (see Note)

¼ cup (56 g) unsalted butter, softened

¾ cup (150 g) granulated sugar

1 egg, at room temperature

1 egg yolk, at room temperature

1 tsp vanilla bean paste or extract

¼ cup (61 g) sour cream, at room temperature

For the Milk Chocolate Malt Buttercream

2 tbsp (30 ml) heavy cream

¼ cup (32 g) malted milk powder, whisked and free of lumps (see Note)

¾ cup (168 g) unsalted butter, softened

⅛ tsp salt

2 oz (56 g) milk chocolate, melted and slightly cooled

5 tbsp (25 g) cocoa powder, scooped and leveled

1½ cups (195 g) powdered sugar

For the Milk Chocolate Ganache

1½ tbsp (22 ml) heavy cream

1½ oz (42 g) milk chocolate, chopped

Chocolate malt balls, for decoration (optional)

To make the chocolate malt cake, preheat the oven to 350°F (177°C). Spray three 4-inch (10-cm) cake pans with nonstick spray, line the bottoms with parchment paper rounds and set aside. In a small bowl, sift together the flour, cocoa powder, baking powder, baking soda, salt and espresso powder (if using), then set aside. In another small bowl, mix the milk and malted milk powder together until dissolved, then set aside.

In a large bowl, cream the butter and granulated sugar together with an electric mixer on high speed for 2 to 3 minutes, until fluffy. Add the egg, egg yolk and vanilla and mix on medium-high speed for 1 to 2 minutes, or until the mixture is pale, smooth and slightly fluffy. Scrape the sides and bottom of the bowl with a spatula as necessary. Then add the malted milk and sour cream and mix on medium speed until combined. The mixture will look curdled at this point, but don't worry.

(continued)

Add the dry ingredients to the wet ingredients a little at a time until all has been added, mixing on low, then medium, speed for each addition. Mix just until the batter is combined and smooth, scraping the sides of the bowl as necessary. The batter will be a little thin.

Divide the batter evenly among the cake pans. Bake the cakes for 28 to 32 minutes, or until a cake tester or toothpick comes out clean from the centers. Let the cakes cool in their pans for 2 minutes, then transfer them to a cooling rack to finish cooling.

Make the milk chocolate malt buttercream while waiting for the cakes to cool. Add the cream to a small bowl and microwave it for 10 to 15 seconds or heat it on the stove in a very small saucepan until steaming, then transfer it to a small bowl. Add the malted milk powder and mix until dissolved, then let it cool completely. Add the butter and salt to a large bowl. Whip with an electric mixer on high speed for 5 to 10 minutes, until the butter is pale, fluffy, and doubled in size. Pour in the melted and slightly cooled milk chocolate and combine on medium speed. Then sift in the cocoa powder and mix on low, then medium, speed until combined. Next, sift the powdered sugar into the mixture ½ cup (65 g) at a time.

Mix on low, then medium, speed, making sure each addition is fully combined before adding the next. Scrape the sides of the bowl as necessary. When the last addition is added, pour in the heavy cream and malted milk mixture and mix on high speed for about 1 minute, until the frosting is light and fluffy.

To make the milk chocolate ganache, add the cream to a small bowl and microwave it for 15 to 25 seconds, or heat it over the stove in a very small saucepan, then transfer it to a small bowl. Add in the chopped milk chocolate, then mix to combine the cream and melted chocolate together. Let the ganache cool to just about room temperature. Stir it while it cools to ensure it cools evenly. Once the ganache is about room temperature, transfer it to a piping bag and cut off a bit of the tip when ready to use.

Please see page 12 for mini cake assembly instructions, using the milk chocolate malt buttercream and milk chocolate ganache when indicated. Decorate with chocolate malt balls (if using), then serve!

I decorated this cake in a naked fashion, but there is enough frosting to fully frost the cake.

Note: This recipe uses non-diastatic malted milk powder. Use a malted milk powder that you would use in a milkshake to flavor it, and not one that you would use as a leavening agent.

Dark Chocolate Cherry Cabernet Cupcakes

We all know chocolate and red wine are basically as essential of a pair as peanut butter and jelly, so I knew these flavors would flourish in cupcake form. These moist dark chocolate cupcakes are filled with a cherry Cabernet reduction and piped to perfection with cherry Cabernet buttercream frosting.

Yield: 12 cupcakes

For the Cherry Cabernet Reduction
9 oz (255 g) pitted cherries
¾ cup (180 ml) Cabernet Sauvignon
6 tbsp (90 g) granulated sugar
1 tbsp (6 g) cornstarch

For the Dark Chocolate Cupcakes
1 cup (125 g) all-purpose flour, spooned and leveled
5 tbsp (25 g) Dutch process cocoa powder, scooped and leveled
½ tsp baking powder
½ tsp baking soda
¼ tsp salt
1 tsp espresso powder (optional)

¼ cup (56 g) unsalted butter, softened
¾ cup (150 g) granulated sugar
1 egg, at room temperature
1 egg yolk, at room temperature
1 tsp vanilla bean paste or extract
½ cup (120 ml) milk, at room temperature
¼ cup (61 g) sour cream, at room temperature

For the Cherry Cabernet Buttercream Frosting
¾ cup (168 g) unsalted butter, softened
⅛ tsp salt
2½ cups (325 g) powdered sugar

12 fresh cherries, for decoration (optional)

Start the cherry Cabernet reduction first. Add the pitted cherries to a blender and blend until they are puréed. Pour the cherry purée into a large saucepan. Add the Cabernet, sugar and cornstarch. Whisk to combine. Simmer over medium heat for 15 to 20 minutes, until the purée has thickened into a jammy consistency. It should coat the back of a spoon thickly. Make sure to watch the reduction and stir it frequently. Remove it from the heat and allow it to cool completely.

To make the dark chocolate cupcakes, preheat the oven to 350°F (177°C). Line a cupcake pan with 12 liners and set aside. In a small bowl, sift together the flour, cocoa powder, baking powder, baking soda, salt and espresso powder (if using), then set aside. Cream the butter and sugar together in a large bowl with an electric mixer on high speed for 2 to 3 minutes, until fluffy. Add the egg, egg yolk and vanilla and mix on medium-high speed for 1 to 2 minutes, or until the mixture is pale, smooth and slightly fluffy. Next, add the milk and sour cream and mix on medium speed until combined. The mixture will look curdled at this point. Add the dry ingredients to the wet ingredients a little at a time until all has been added, mixing on low, then medium, speed for each addition. Mix just until the batter is combined and smooth. The batter will be a little thin. Divide the batter evenly among the 12 liners until each is about three-quarters full. Bake the cupcakes for 16 to 19 minutes, or until a cake tester or toothpick comes out clean from the centers. Let the cupcakes cool in the pan for 10 minutes, then transfer them to a cooling rack to finish cooling.

To make the cherry Cabernet buttercream, add the butter and salt to a large bowl. Whip it with an electric mixer on high speed for 5 to 10 minutes, until the butter is pale, fluffy and doubled in size. Sift the powdered sugar into the mixture 1 cup (130 g) or so at a time. Mix on low, then medium, speed, making sure each addition is fully combined before adding the next. Add ¼ cup (60 ml) of the cherry Cabernet reduction and mix the frosting for 1 minute or so until it is light and fluffy. Transfer the frosting to a piping bag fitted with a decorative tip.

Please see page 15 for filled cupcake assembly instructions. Top with a cherry (if using), then serve!

White Chocolate Macadamia Nut Cupcakes

By far my favorite cookies are white chocolate macadamia nut, so I just had to make them into a cupcake! These brown sugar vanilla cupcakes have chopped macadamia nuts throughout and are topped with my all-time favorite: white chocolate buttercream. Each bite is full of toasty notes of macadamia nut and sweet, melt-in-your-mouth white chocolate. If you're a white chocolate macadamia fan, I know these will be your new favorite!

Yield: 12 cupcakes

For the Cupcakes

1 cup + 2 tbsp (141 g) all-purpose flour, spooned and leveled

¾ tsp baking powder

⅛ tsp baking soda

¼ tsp salt

5 tbsp (70 g) unsalted butter, softened

½ cup (100 g) granulated sugar

¼ cup (55 g) light brown sugar, packed

1 egg, at room temperature

1 egg yolk, at room temperature

1 tsp vanilla bean paste or extract

½ cup (120 ml) buttermilk, at room temperature

¼ cup (35 g) macadamia nuts, coarsely chopped

For the White Chocolate Buttercream

¾ cup (168 grams) unsalted butter, softened

⅛ tsp salt

3 oz (85 g) white chocolate, melted and slightly cooled

1½ cups (195 g) powdered sugar

Macadamia nuts, for topping (optional)

To make the cupcakes, preheat the oven to 350°F (177°C). Line a cupcake pan with 12 liners. In a small bowl, sift together the flour, baking powder, baking soda and salt, then set aside. In a large bowl, cream the butter, granulated sugar and brown sugar together with an electric mixer on high for 2 to 3 minutes, until fluffy. Add the egg, egg yolk and vanilla and mix on medium-high speed for 1 to 2 minutes, or until the mixture is pale and smooth. Scrape the sides and bottom of the bowl with a spatula as necessary.

Alternate adding the dry ingredients and the buttermilk to the butter mixture a little at a time until each has been completely incorporated, mixing on low, then medium, speed for each addition. Mix just until the batter is combined and smooth, scraping the sides of the bowl as necessary. Lastly add in the chopped macadamia nuts and mix on low speed until evenly distributed throughout the batter.

Divide the batter evenly among the 12 liners until each is about three-quarters full. Bake the cupcakes for 17 to 20 minutes, or until a cake tester or toothpick comes out clean from the centers. Let the cupcakes cool in their pan for 10 minutes, then transfer them to a cooling rack to finish cooling.

Make the white chocolate buttercream while waiting for the cupcakes to cool. Add the butter and salt to a large bowl. Whip with an electric mixer on high speed for 5 to 10 minutes, until the butter is pale, fluffy and doubled in size. Pour in the melted and slightly cooled white chocolate and combine on medium speed. Then sift the powdered sugar into the mixture ½ cup (65 g) at a time.

Mix on low, then medium, speed, making sure each addition is fully combined before adding the next. Scrape the sides of the bowl as necessary. When the last addition is incorporated, mix on high speed for about 1 minute, until the frosting is light and fluffy. Transfer the frosting to a piping bag fitted with a decorative tip.

Once the cupcakes are completely cooled, pipe a generous amount of frosting onto each and top with extra macadamia nuts (if using), then serve!

Dark Chocolate Mint Cupcakes

As an ice cream flavor chocolate and mint are a match made in heaven, and in cupcake form even more so. These dark chocolate cupcakes are exceptionally moist, with hints of cool peppermint throughout. They're frosted with a perfect pairing of minty cream cheese frosting. Be sure to add a sprinkle of dark chocolate shavings for an aesthetically pleasing touch.

Yield: 12 cupcakes

For the Dark Chocolate Mint Cupcakes

1 cup (125 g) all-purpose flour, spooned and leveled

5 tbsp (25 g) Dutch process cocoa powder, scooped and leveled

½ tsp baking powder

½ tsp baking soda

¼ tsp salt

1 tsp espresso powder (optional)

¼ cup (56 g) unsalted butter, softened

¾ cup (150 g) granulated sugar

1 egg, at room temperature

1 egg yolk, at room temperature

1 tsp vanilla bean paste or extract

1 tsp peppermint extract

½ cup (120 ml) milk, at room temperature

¼ cup (61 g) sour cream, at room temperature

For the Mint Cream Cheese Frosting

½ cup (112 g) unsalted butter, softened

4 oz (113 g) cream cheese, cold

2 cups (260 g) powdered sugar

½ tsp peppermint extract

3–4 drops green food coloring (optional)

Chocolate shavings, for decoration (optional)

To make the dark chocolate cupcakes, preheat the oven to 350°F (177°C). Line a cupcake pan with 12 liners and set aside. In a small bowl, sift together the flour, cocoa powder, baking powder, baking soda, salt and espresso powder (if using), then set aside. Cream the butter and sugar together in a large bowl with an electric mixer on high speed for 2 to 3 minutes until fluffy. Add the egg, egg yolk, vanilla and peppermint extract and mix on medium-high for 1 to 2 minutes, or until the mixture is pale, smooth and slightly fluffy.

Next, add the milk and sour cream and mix on medium speed until combined. The mixture will look curdled at this point, but don't worry. Add the dry ingredients to the wet ingredients a little at a time until all has been added, mixing on low, then medium, speed for each addition. Mix just until the batter is combined and smooth, scraping the sides of the bowl as necessary. The batter will be a little thin.

Divide the batter evenly among the 12 liners until each is about three-quarters full. Bake the cupcakes for 16 to 19 minutes, or until a cake tester or toothpick comes out clean from the centers. Let the cupcakes cool in the pan for 10 minutes, then transfer them to a cooling rack to finish cooling.

Make the mint cream cheese frosting while waiting for the cupcakes to cool. Add the butter to a large bowl and whip with an electric mixer on high speed for 5 to 10 minutes, until it is pale, fluffy and doubled in size. Add the cream cheese and mix on medium-high speed until thoroughly combined.

Next, sift the powdered sugar into the mixture 1 cup (130 g) at a time. Mix on low, then medium, speed, making sure the first addition is fully combined before adding the next. When the last addition is incorporated, add the peppermint extract and green food coloring (if using) and mix on medium, then high, speed for about 1 minute, until the frosting is light and fluffy. Transfer the frosting to a piping bag fitted with a decorative tip.

When the cupcakes are completely cooled, pipe a generous amount of frosting onto each. Sprinkle with chocolate shavings (if using), then serve!

White Chocolate Raspberry Cupcakes

White chocolate raspberry has quickly become a very common flavor pairing, and for good reason. The tartness of the raspberries and the light sweetness of the white chocolate work so well together. These tender cupcakes use freeze-dried raspberries to really pack in the raspberry flavor without all the excess moisture of fresh raspberries. After baking they're piped with silky smooth white chocolate buttercream. Top them with a raspberry and white chocolate for an elegant touch.

Yield: 12 cupcakes

For the Raspberry Cupcakes
½ cup (12 g) whole freeze-dried raspberries

1¼ cups (140 g) cake flour, spooned and leveled

¾ tsp baking powder

⅛ tsp baking soda

¼ tsp salt

5 tbsp (70 g) unsalted butter, softened

¾ cup (150 g) granulated sugar

2 egg whites, at room temperature

1 tsp vanilla bean paste or extract

½ cup (120 ml) buttermilk, at room temperature

2–3 drops pink food coloring (optional)

For the White Chocolate Buttercream
¾ cup (168 g) unsalted butter, softened

⅛ tsp salt

3 oz (85 g) white chocolate, melted and slightly cooled

1½ cups (195 g) powdered sugar

12 raspberries, for decoration (optional)

12 white chocolate pieces, for decoration (optional)

For the raspberry cupcakes, preheat the oven to 350°F (177°C). Line a cupcake pan with 12 liners and set aside. Place the freeze-dried raspberries in a baggie. Using a rolling pin, crush the raspberries until they are very finely ground. Keep the raspberries in the bag until ready to add to the batter so that they stay dry.

In a small bowl, sift together the cake flour, baking powder, baking soda and salt, then set aside. In a large bowl, cream the butter and sugar together with an electric mixer on high speed for 2 to 3 minutes, until fluffy. Add the egg whites and vanilla and mix on medium-high speed for 1 to 2 minutes, until pale and smooth.

Alternate adding the dry ingredients and the buttermilk to the butter mixture a little at a time until each has been added completely, mixing on low, then medium, speed for each addition. Mix just until the batter is combined and smooth. Then add the freeze-dried raspberries and a few drops of pink coloring (if using) to the batter. Mix on medium-low speed just until combined.

Divide the batter evenly among the 12 liners. Each should be two-thirds to three-quarters of the way full. Bake the cupcakes for 15 to 18 minutes, or until a cake tester or toothpick comes out clean from the centers. Let the cupcakes cool in the pan for 10 minutes, then transfer them to a cooling rack to finish cooling.

To make the white chocolate buttercream, add the butter and salt to a large bowl. Whip it with an electric mixer on high speed for 5 to 10 minutes, until the butter is pale, fluffy and doubled in size. Add the white chocolate and combine on medium speed. Sift the powdered sugar into the mixture ½ cup (65 g) at a time. Mix on low, then medium, speed, making sure each addition is fully combined before adding the next. When the last addition is added, mix on high speed for about 1 minute, until the frosting is light and fluffy. Transfer the frosting to a piping bag fitted with a decorative tip.

Once the cupcakes are cooled, pipe a generous amount of frosting onto each. Top with raspberries and white chocolate (if using), then serve!

Vintage Varieties

This timeless chapter takes a moment to admire some of the best classic desserts of all time. In this section, older, retro desserts are reimagined into mini cakes and cupcakes. It was so enjoyable to take these lasting recipes and create something totally new. Here you'll find recipes such as Key Lime Pie Mini Cake (page 48), Bananas Foster Cupcakes (page 57), Coconut Cream Pie Cupcakes (page 67) and Tiramisu Cupcakes (page 47). These everlasting recipes will captivate your heart and palate as you savor every delectable bite.

Tiramisu Cupcakes

Traditionally, tiramisu is made up of layers of lady fingers soaked in coffee liqueur or Marsala wine and sweet mascarpone whipped cream. This recipe transforms the classic dessert into the cutest cupcakes! Light, fluffy, sweet mascarpone whipped cream frosting sits atop the softest coffee-soaked white cupcakes. They're then finished with a dusting of cocoa powder. These pretty cupcakes are fancy and easy at the same time!

Yield: 12 cupcakes

For the White Cupcakes
1¼ cups (140 g) cake flour, spooned and leveled

¾ tsp baking powder

⅛ tsp baking soda

¼ tsp salt

5 tbsp (70 g) unsalted butter, softened

¾ cup (150 g) granulated sugar

2 egg whites, room temperature

1½ tsp (8 ml) vanilla bean paste or extract

½ cup (120 ml) buttermilk, at room temperature

For the Coffee Soak
½ cup (120 ml) brewed coffee, hot

¼ cup (50 g) granulated sugar

2 tbsp (30 ml) Marsala wine or Kahlúa® (optional)

For the Mascarpone Whipped Cream
½ cup (120 ml) heavy whipping cream, cold

8 oz (226 g) mascarpone cheese, cold

1 tsp vanilla bean paste or extract

½ cup (65 g) powdered sugar

Cocoa powder, for dusting

To make the white cupcakes, preheat the oven to 350°F (177°C). Line a cupcake pan with 12 liners and set aside. In a small bowl, sift together the cake flour, baking powder, baking soda and salt, then set aside. In a large bowl, cream the butter and sugar together with an electric mixer on high speed for 2 to 3 minutes, until it is light and fluffy. Next, add the egg whites and vanilla and mix on medium-high speed for 1 to 2 minutes, until pale and smooth. Alternate adding the dry ingredients and the buttermilk to the butter mixture a little at a time until each has been added completely, mixing on low, then medium, speed for each addition. Mix just until the batter is combined and smooth. The batter will be thick.

Divide the batter evenly among the 12 liners until each is two-thirds to three-quarters full. Bake the cupcakes for 16 to 18 minutes, or until a cake tester or toothpick comes out clean from the centers. Let the cupcakes cool in the pan for 10 minutes, then transfer them to a cooling rack to finish cooling.

To make the coffee soak, mix the hot coffee and sugar together in a small bowl until all the sugar is dissolved. Then mix in the Marsala wine or Kahlúa (if using) and let the mixture cool completely. When the cupcakes are completely cooled, poke holes liberally in their tops using a toothpick. Slowly drizzle about 2 teaspoons (10 ml) of the coffee soak over each cupcake, and wait until all the liquid is absorbed.

Make the mascarpone whipped cream by adding the heavy whipping cream to a chilled bowl. Whip the cream with an electric mixer on high speed for 1 to 2 minutes, until stiff peaks form. To a separate medium-sized bowl, add the mascarpone cheese and vanilla. Sift in the powdered sugar, then mix with an electric mixer on medium speed for 1 to 2 minutes, until smooth and fluffy. Gently fold the whipped cream into the mascarpone mixture with a spatula until everything is combined. Transfer the frosting to a piping bag fitted with a decorative tip.

Pipe a generous portion of the mascarpone whipped cream onto the tops of each cupcake. Dust each with cocoa powder, then serve!

Key Lime Pie Mini Cake

Living in Florida my whole life, Key lime pie has been an essential part of my existence. We even had a Key lime tree in our yard, which my dad tended to like it was his second child. Our family has a delicious Key lime pie recipe that is the inspiration behind this cake. Here, the crust of the pie takes form in fluffy vanilla graham cracker cake layers. The filling of the pie is showcased as a Key lime juice reduction cream cheese frosting. The tart, creamy frosting contrasts beautifully with the soft vanilla graham cracker cake in a way I know all Key lime pie fans will adore! This recipe is dedicated to my dad, Ray, who loves Key lime pie as much as I do.

Yield: 1 (4-inch [10-cm]) three-tier cake

For the Vanilla Graham Cracker Cake

¾ cup (94 g) all-purpose flour, spooned and leveled

⅓ cup (34 g) graham cracker crumbs, very finely ground

¾ tsp baking powder

⅛ tsp baking soda

¼ tsp salt

5 tbsp (70 g) unsalted butter, softened

½ cup (100 g) granulated sugar

¼ cup (55 g) light brown sugar, packed

1 egg, at room temperature

1 egg yolk, at room temperature

1 tsp vanilla bean paste or extract

½ cup (120 ml) buttermilk, at room temperature

For the Key Lime Cream Cheese Frosting

½ cup (120 ml) Key lime juice, bottled or fresh

½ cup (112 g) unsalted butter, softened

4 oz (114 g) cream cheese, cold

2½ cups (325 g) powdered sugar

To make the vanilla graham cracker cake, preheat the oven to 350°F (177°C). Spray three 4-inch (10-cm) cake pans with nonstick spray and line the bottoms with parchment paper rounds. In a small bowl, whisk together the flour, graham cracker crumbs, baking powder, baking soda and salt, then set aside. In a large bowl, cream the butter, granulated sugar and brown sugar together with an electric mixer on high speed for 2 to 3 minutes, until fluffy. Add the egg, egg yolk and vanilla and mix on medium-high speed for 1 to 2 minutes, until the mixture is pale and smooth. Scrape the sides and bottom of the bowl with a spatula as necessary.

Alternate adding the dry ingredients and the buttermilk to the butter mixture a little at a time until each has been added completely, mixing on low, then medium, speed for each addition. Mix just until the batter is combined and smooth, scraping the sides of the bowl as necessary. Divide the batter evenly among the cake pans. Bake the cakes for 25 to 28 minutes, or until a cake tester or toothpick comes out clean from the centers. Let the cakes cool in their pans for 2 minutes, then transfer them to a cooling rack to finish cooling.

Make the Key lime reduction for the frosting while the cakes bake by pouring the Key lime juice into a small saucepan. Heat the juice over medium-high heat for about 15 minutes, until it reduces to 1 tablespoon (15 ml). Stir it frequently as it simmers. Remove it from the heat and allow it to cool completely while working on the rest of the frosting.

To make the Key lime cream cheese frosting, add the butter to a large bowl. Whip with an electric mixer for 5 to 10 minutes, until the butter is pale, fluffy and doubled in size. Add the cream cheese and mix on medium-high speed until thoroughly combined. Next, sift the powdered sugar into the mixture 1 cup (130 g) at a time. Mix on low, then medium, speed, making sure each addition is fully combined before adding the next. When the last addition is added, pour in the cooled Key lime juice reduction and mix on medium, then high, speed for about 1 minute, until the frosting is light and fluffy.

Please see page 12 for mini cake assembly instructions, using the Key lime cream cheese frosting, then serve. I frosted this cake in a naked fashion, but there is enough frosting to cover the entire cake.

Cinnamon Peach Cobbler Cupcakes

Whether you get your peaches out in Georgia or not, can we agree that peach cobbler with vanilla ice cream in the summertime is everything? This classic dessert was re-created in these fluffy cinnamon cupcakes filled with a delicious spiced-peach compote. After baking, the cupcakes are topped with a swirl of creamy vanilla cinnamon cream cheese frosting.

Yield: 12 cupcakes

For the Peach Filling
2 cups (10 oz [284 g]) fresh peaches, unpeeled, sliced and cut into 1-inch (2.5-cm) pieces

¼ cup (50 g) granulated sugar

½ tsp cinnamon

¼ tsp nutmeg

1 tsp vanilla bean paste or extract

1 tsp cornstarch

For the Cinnamon Cupcakes
1 cup + 2 tbsp (141 g) all-purpose flour, spooned and leveled

1½ tsp (4 g) cinnamon

¾ tsp baking powder

⅛ tsp baking soda

¼ tsp salt

5 tbsp (70 g) unsalted butter, softened

¾ cup (150 g) granulated sugar

1 egg, at room temperature

1 egg yolk, at room temperature

1 tsp vanilla bean paste or extract

½ cup (120 ml) buttermilk, at room temperature

For the Vanilla Cinnamon Cream Cheese Frosting
½ cup (112 g) unsalted butter, softened

4 oz (114 g) cream cheese, cold

2 cups (260 g) powdered sugar, sifted

1½ tsp (4 g) cinnamon

1 tsp vanilla bean paste or extract

Make the peach filling first so it has plenty of time to cool. Add the peaches to a small saucepan. Sprinkle the sugar, cinnamon, nutmeg, vanilla and cornstarch over them. Stir to evenly coat the peaches. Cook the peaches over medium-low heat for about 20 minutes, until the juice has thickened, stirring frequently. Remove the peaches from the heat and allow them to cool completely.

To make the cinnamon cupcakes, preheat the oven to 350°F (177°C). Line a cupcake pan with 12 liners. In a small bowl, sift together the flour, cinnamon, baking powder, baking soda and salt, then set aside. In a large bowl, cream the butter and granulated sugar together with an electric mixer on high speed for 2 to 3 minutes, until fluffy. Add the egg, egg yolk and vanilla and mix on medium-high speed for 1 to 2 minutes, or until the mixture is pale, smooth and slightly fluffy. Scrape the sides and bottom of the bowl with a spatula as necessary.

Alternate adding the dry ingredients and the buttermilk to the butter mixture a little at a time until each has been added completely, mixing on low, then medium, speed for each addition. Mix just until the batter is combined and smooth, scraping the sides and bottom of the bowl as necessary.

Divide the batter evenly among the 12 liners until each is two-thirds to three-quarters full. Bake the cupcakes for 17 to 20 minutes, or until a cake tester or toothpick comes out clean from the centers. Let the cupcakes cool in their pan for 10 minutes, then transfer them to a cooling rack to finish cooling.

(continued)

Make the vanilla cinnamon cream cheese frosting while the cupcakes cool. Add the butter to a large bowl and whip it with an electric mixer for 5 to 10 minutes, until it is pale, fluffy and has doubled in size. Add in the cream cheese and mix on medium-high speed until thoroughly combined.

Next, sift the powdered sugar into the mixture 1 cup (130 g) at a time. Mix on low, then medium, speed, making sure the first addition is fully combined before adding the last. When the last addition is incorporated, add in the cinnamon and vanilla and mix on medium, then high, speed for about 1 minute, until the frosting is light and fluffy.

Please see page 15 for filled cupcake assembly instructions, using the peach filling and vanilla cinnamon cream cheese frosting when indicated, then serve and enjoy!

Dulce de Leche Churro Mini Cake

Not only is this cake a total show-stopper, it tastes even better than it looks! Layers of fluffy cinnamon cake are rolled in cinnamon sugar to look like a churro and filled with silky dulce de leche buttercream. The cake is finished with a dulce de leche drip for a special, delicious touch.

Fun Fact: Did you know that churros are a very old dessert, as in from the sixteenth century? I truly had no idea! I thought they were a fairly modern dessert and had originally planned to include this cake in a different chapter. It turns out, churros are the most vintage of all the desserts in this entire section!

Yield: 1 (4-inch [10-cm]) three-tier cake

For the Dulce de Leche
1 (14-oz [400-g]) can of sweetened condensed milk

For the Cinnamon Cake
1 cup + 2 tbsp (141 g) all-purpose flour, spooned and leveled

2 tsp (5 g) cinnamon

¾ tsp baking powder

⅛ tsp baking soda

¼ tsp salt

5 tbsp (70 g) unsalted butter, softened

½ cup (100 g) granulated sugar

¼ cup (55 g) light brown sugar, packed

1 egg, at room temperature

1 egg yolk, at room temperature

½ tsp vanilla extract

½ cup (120 ml) buttermilk, at room temperature

For the Dulce de Leche Buttercream
¾ cup (168 g) unsalted butter, softened

¼ tsp salt

1 cup (130 g) powdered sugar

For the Cinnamon Sugar Coating
¼ cup (50 g) granulated sugar

½ tsp cinnamon

2 tbsp (28 g) unsalted butter, melted

Churros, for decoration (optional)

To make the dulce de leche, add a sealed can of sweetened condensed milk to a pot of water, making sure the can is completely submerged with at least 2 inches (5 cm) of water over it. Bring the water to a boil, then turn the heat down to low and let the water simmer for 2 hours and 45 minutes. Add more water as necessary to always keep at least 2 inches (5 cm) of water over the can. Halfway through, using tongs, turn the can upside down to ensure the sweetened condensed milk gets heated evenly. After 2 hours and 45 minutes, remove the sweetened condensed milk from the pot and allow it to cool completely before opening it, around 2 hours.

To make the cinnamon cake, preheat the oven to 350°F (177°C). Spray three 4-inch (10-cm) cake pans with nonstick spray, then set aside. In a small bowl, sift together the all-purpose flour, cinnamon, baking powder, baking soda and salt, then set aside. In a large bowl, cream the butter, granulated sugar and brown sugar together with an electric mixer on high speed for 2 to 3 minutes, until fluffy. Add the egg, egg yolk and vanilla and mix on medium-high speed for 1 to 2 minutes, or until the mixture is smooth and pale. Scrape the sides and bottom of the bowl with a spatula as necessary.

(continued)

Alternate adding the dry ingredients and the buttermilk to the butter mixture a little at a time until each has been added completely, mixing on low, then medium, speed for each addition. Mix just until the batter is combined and smooth, scraping the sides of the bowl as necessary.

Divide the batter evenly among the cake pans. Bake the cakes for 24 to 27 minutes, or until a cake tester or toothpick comes out clean from the centers. Let the cakes cool in their pans for 2 minutes, then transfer them to a cooling rack to finish cooling.

To make the dulce de leche buttercream, add the butter and salt to a large bowl. Whip it with an electric mixer on high speed for 5 to 10 minutes, until the butter is pale, fluffy, and doubled in size. Add ¾ cup (234 g) of the prepared dulce de leche and mix on medium speed until combined. Sift the powdered sugar into the mixture and mix on medium speed until combined. Then mix on high speed for about 1 minute, until the frosting is light and fluffy. Transfer the dulce de leche buttercream to a piping bag fitted with a decorative tip. This frosting is a little softer than most, so you may need to refrigerate it for 10 to 15 minutes after making it and then re-whip it so it's a little more stable.

To make the cinnamon sugar coating, whisk the sugar and cinnamon together in a medium-sized shallow bowl. Melt the butter and add it to a small bowl.

To assemble the churro cake, you'll first want to make sure the cake layers are even and have a flat top so that they stack properly. With a sharp knife cut each domed top off so that each layer is even. Brush the outside edges of each cake layer with the melted butter and roll each in the cinnamon sugar. Pipe swirls of frosting onto the first cake layer, starting at the edges and working your way in. Then place the next layer over top and repeat the step. Place the final layer on top. Add the remaining dulce de leche to a piping bag and cut just a little bit of the tip off. Go around the edges of the top of the cake and pipe dulce de leche on just until it begins to drip, spacing your drips out about every quarter- to half-inch (6-mm to 1-cm). Then with the remaining frosting, pipe decorative swirls on top of the cake. Top with churros (if using), then serve the cake! Drizzle extra dulce de leche on each slice of cake if you desire.

Bananas Foster Cupcakes

Bananas foster is a classic dessert and these bananas foster cupcakes taste just like the real deal! Soft and fluffy banana spice cupcakes are topped with a banana spice buttercream and drizzled with a boozy brown sugar caramel rum sauce. Top them with a banana slice for a cute touch!

Yield: 12 cupcakes

For the Banana Spice Cupcakes
1 cup + 2 tbsp (141 g) all-purpose flour, spooned and leveled

½ tsp cinnamon

¾ tsp baking powder

⅛ tsp baking soda

¼ tsp salt

5 tbsp (70 g) unsalted butter, softened

¾ cup (150 g) granulated sugar

1 egg, at room temperature

1 egg yolk, at room temperature

1 tsp vanilla bean paste or extract

¼ cup (60 ml) buttermilk, at room temperature

½ cup (125 g) mashed banana

For the Caramel Rum Sauce
¼ cup (55 g) light brown sugar, packed

2 tbsp (28 g) salted butter

2 tbsp (30 ml) dark rum

For the Banana Spice Buttercream
¾ cup (168 g) unsalted butter, softened

⅛ tsp salt

3 tbsp (46 g) mashed banana

2 cups (260 g) powdered sugar

1 tsp cinnamon

12 banana slices, for decoration (optional)

To make the banana spice cupcakes, preheat the oven to 350°F (177°C). Line a cupcake pan with 12 liners and set aside. In a small bowl, whisk together the flour, cinnamon, baking powder, baking soda and salt, then set aside. In a large bowl, cream the butter and sugar together with an electric mixer on high speed for 2 to 3 minutes, until it is light and fluffy. Add the egg, egg yolk and vanilla and mix on medium-high speed for 1 to 2 minutes, until pale, smooth and slightly fluffy, 1 to 2 minutes. Add half the dry ingredients and the buttermilk to the butter mixture and mix on low, then medium, speed until combined. Add the mashed banana and the rest of the dry ingredients. Mix on low, then medium, speed until the batter is combined and smooth, scraping the sides of the bowl as necessary.

Divide the batter evenly among the 12 liners until each is two-thirds to three-quarters full. Bake the cupcakes for 17 to 19 minutes, or until a cake tester or toothpick comes out clean from the centers. Let the cupcakes cool in the pan for 10 minutes, then transfer them to a cooling rack to finish cooling.

Make the caramel rum sauce while the cupcakes cool by adding the brown sugar, salted butter and rum to a small saucepan. Bring the mixture to a simmer over medium-low heat. Let the mixture simmer for 30 seconds, then remove it from the heat and allow it to cool completely.

Make the banana spice buttercream while waiting for the caramel rum sauce to cool. Add the butter and salt to a large bowl and whip it with an electric mixer on high for 5 to 10 minutes, until it is pale, fluffy and has doubled in size. Add the mashed banana and mix on medium speed until combined. Next, sift the powdered sugar into the mixture 1 cup (130 g) at a time. Mix on low, then medium, speed, making sure the first addition is fully combined before adding the last. When the last addition is incorporated, add the cinnamon and mix on medium, then high, speed for about 1 minute, until the frosting is light and fluffy. Transfer the frosting to a piping bag fitted with a decorative tip.

When the cupcakes are completely cooled, pipe a generous amount of frosting onto each. Drizzle the caramel rum sauce over them, top with a slice of banana (if using) and serve!

Pineapple Upside Down Cupcakes

Pineapple upside down cake is such a fun, retro dessert with just the best flavor. That classic yellow cake and pineapple combo is so nostalgic for me. The dessert has been reimagined with this recipe to be vanilla pineapple cupcakes soaked with a pineapple caramel sauce, like the sauce that forms when baking the traditional dessert. The cupcakes are topped with a smooth and tangy pineapple buttercream and garnished with a pineapple slice and maraschino cherry. Okay, they're technically not upside down, but all the flavors of the classic dessert are here!

Yield: 12 cupcakes

For the Vanilla Pineapple Cupcakes

1 cup + 2 tbsp (141 g) all-purpose flour, spooned and leveled

¾ tsp baking powder

⅛ tsp baking soda

¼ tsp salt

5 tbsp (70 g) unsalted butter, softened

¾ cup (150 g) granulated sugar

1 egg, at room temperature

1 egg yolk, at room temperature

1 tsp vanilla bean paste or extract

⅓ cup (80 ml) buttermilk, at room temperature

⅓ cup (75 g) crushed canned pineapple, strained with juice reserved for caramel sauce and frosting

For the Pineapple Caramel Sauce

⅓ cup (80 ml) pineapple juice

¼ cup (55 g) brown sugar, packed

For the Pineapple Buttercream

¾ cup (168 g) unsalted butter, softened

⅛ tsp salt

2 cups (260 g) powdered sugar

3 tbsp (45 ml) pineapple juice

12 pineapple slices, for garnish (optional)

12 maraschino cherries, for garnish (optional)

To make the vanilla pineapple cupcakes, preheat the oven to 350°F (177°C). Line a cupcake pan with 12 liners and set aside. In a small bowl, whisk together the flour, baking powder, baking soda and salt, then set aside. In a large bowl, cream the butter and sugar together with an electric mixer on high speed for 2 to 3 minutes, until it is light and fluffy. Add the egg, egg yolk and vanilla and mix on medium-high speed for 1 to 2 minutes, until pale, smooth and slightly fluffy. Scrape the sides and bottom of the bowl with a spatula as necessary.

Alternate adding the dry ingredients and the buttermilk to the butter mixture a little at a time until each has been added completely, mixing on low, then medium, speed for each addition. Mix just until the batter is combined and smooth, scraping the sides of the bowl as necessary. Lastly, add the strained, crushed pineapple and mix on low speed just until combined.

Divide the batter evenly among the 12 liners until each is two-thirds to three-quarters full. Bake the cupcakes for 17 to 19 minutes, or until a cake tester or toothpick comes out clean from the centers. Let the cupcakes cool in the pan for 10 minutes, then transfer them to a cooling rack to finish cooling.

(continued)

Make the pineapple caramel sauce while the cupcakes bake by adding the pineapple juice and brown sugar to a small saucepan. Whisk to combine, then bring the mixture to a simmer over medium-low heat. Let the mixture simmer until slightly thicker, about 3 minutes. Remove from the heat and transfer to a small bowl. Allow the sauce to cool completely before using it on the cupcakes.

Make the pineapple buttercream while the cupcakes cool. Add the butter and salt to a large bowl and whip it with an electric mixer on high speed for 5 to 10 minutes, until it is pale, fluffy and has doubled in size. Sift the powdered sugar into the mixture 1 cup (130 g) at a time. Mix on low, then medium, speed, making sure the first addition is fully combined before adding the last. Scrape the sides of the bowl as necessary. Next, add the pineapple juice and mix on medium speed until combined. Then mix the frosting on high speed for about 1 minute, until it is light and fluffy. Transfer the frosting to a piping bag fitted with a decorative tip.

When the cupcakes are completely cooled, poke holes liberally in their tops using a toothpick. Slowly drizzle about 1 teaspoon of pineapple caramel sauce on top of each, and wait for it to all soak in. Place a pineapple ring on top (if using), then pipe a generous amount of frosting on top of each cupcake. Top each with a maraschino cherry (if using) and serve!

Blueberry Cobbler Mini Cake

Blueberry cobbler is such a timeless comfort food, with its bursting sweetened blueberry filling and buttery, sweet cake crumb topping. This cake is inspired by my grandma's out-of-this-world blueberry cobbler. The dessert is adapted here to be a buttery brown sugar vanilla cake filled with a thick blueberry compote. It's frosted with luscious cream cheese frosting and a swirl of blueberry. The cake is topped with more blueberry compote and a sprinkle of cake crumbs. If you love blueberry cobbler, this cake is going to be your new favorite. This recipe is dedicated to Elsie and Lisa, who taught me how to make the best cobbler.

Yield: 1 (4-inch [10-cm]) three-tier cake

For the Blueberry Compote
12 oz (340 g) fresh blueberries
½ cup (100 g) granulated sugar
2 tbsp (16 g) cornstarch, scooped and leveled
1 tsp vanilla bean paste or extract

For the Brown Sugar Vanilla Butter Cake
1 cup + 2 tbsp (141 g) all-purpose flour, spooned and leveled
¾ tsp baking powder
⅛ tsp baking soda
¼ tsp salt
5 tbsp (70 g) unsalted butter, softened

½ cup (100 g) granulated sugar
¼ cup (55 g) light brown sugar
1 egg, at room temperature
1 egg yolk, at room temperature
1 tsp vanilla bean paste or extract
½ tsp butter extract (optional)
½ cup (120 ml) buttermilk, at room temperature

For the Cream Cheese Frosting
½ cup (112 g) unsalted butter, softened
4 oz (114 g) cream cheese, cold
2 cups (260 g) powdered sugar
1 tsp vanilla bean paste or extract

Start the blueberry compote first so it has plenty of time to cool. Add the blueberries, sugar, cornstarch and vanilla to a large saucepan over medium-low heat. Slightly mash the berries with the back of a wooden spoon and stir to combine everything. Let the berries simmer and thicken for about 20 minutes. Remove the compote from the heat and allow it to cool completely. This recipe will make about ¾ cup (180 ml) of blueberry compote.

To make the brown sugar vanilla butter cake, preheat the oven to 350°F (177°C). Spray three 4-inch (10-cm) cake pans with nonstick spray and line the bottoms with parchment paper rounds. In a small bowl, sift together the all-purpose flour, baking powder, baking soda and salt, then set aside. In a large bowl, cream the butter, granulated sugar and light brown sugar together with an electric mixer on high for 2 to 3 minutes, until fluffy. Add the egg, egg yolk, vanilla and butter extract (if using) and mix on medium-high speed for 1 to 2 minutes, or until the mixture is pale and smooth.

Alternate adding the dry ingredients and the buttermilk to the butter mixture a little at a time, until each has been added completely, mixing on low, then medium, speed for each addition. Mix just until the batter is combined and smooth, scraping the sides of the bowl with a spatula as necessary.

Divide the batter evenly among the cake pans. Bake the cakes for 26 to 30 minutes, or until a cake tester or toothpick comes out clean from the centers. Let the cakes cool in their pans for 2 minutes, then transfer them to a cooling rack to finish cooling.

(continued)

Make the cream cheese frosting while waiting for the cakes to cool. Add the butter to a large bowl. Whip with an electric mixer on high speed for 5 to 10 minutes, until the butter is pale, fluffy and doubled in size. Add the cream cheese and mix on medium-high speed until thoroughly combined.

Next, sift the powdered sugar into the mixture 1 cup (130 g) at a time. Mix on low, then medium, speed, making sure the first addition is fully combined before adding the last. When the last addition is incorporated, add in the vanilla and mix on medium, then high, speed for about 1 minute, until the frosting is light and fluffy.

Please see page 12 for mini cake assembly instructions, using the blueberry compote filling and cream cheese frosting when indicated. Reserve some of the cake top crumbs for sprinkling over the assembled cake and some of the compote for swirling on the outside of the cake (optional), then serve and enjoy!

Hummingbird Cupcakes

This classic southern US dessert is one that I have completely fallen in love with. These moist and tender cinnamon-spiced pineapple-banana cupcakes have chopped pecans mixed throughout and are topped with a simple yet delicious cream cheese frosting. They are easy to make, super tender, and each bite truly just melts in your mouth!

Yield: 12 cupcakes

For the Hummingbird Cupcakes

1 cup + 2 tbsp (141 g) all-purpose flour, spooned and leveled

1 tsp cinnamon

¾ tsp baking powder

⅛ tsp baking soda

¼ tsp salt

5 tbsp (70 g) unsalted butter, softened

¾ cup (150 g) granulated sugar

1 egg, at room temperature

1 egg yolk, at room temperature

1 tsp vanilla bean paste or extract

¼ cup (60 ml) buttermilk, at room temperature

¼ cup (55 g) crushed canned pineapple, drained

¼ cup (63 g) mashed banana

¼ cup (28 g) chopped pecans, plus more for topping

For the Cream Cheese Frosting

½ cup (112 g) unsalted butter, softened

4 oz (114 g) cream cheese, cold

2 cups (260 g) powdered sugar, sifted

To make the hummingbird cupcakes, preheat the oven to 350°F (177°C). Line a cupcake pan with 12 liners and set aside. In a small bowl, whisk together the flour, cinnamon, baking powder, baking soda and salt, then set aside. In a large bowl, cream the butter and sugar together with an electric mixer on high speed for 2 to 3 minutes, until it is fluffy. Add the egg, egg yolk and vanilla and mix on medium-high speed for 1 to 2 minutes, until pale, smooth and slightly fluffy. Scrape the sides and bottom of the bowl with a spatula as necessary.

Add half the dry ingredients and the buttermilk to the butter mixture and mix on low, then medium, speed until combined. Then add the drained crushed pineapple, mashed banana and the rest of the dry ingredients, and mix on low, then medium, speed until the batter is combined, scraping the sides of the bowl as necessary. Add the chopped pecans and mix on low speed just until combined.

Divide the batter evenly among the 12 liners until each is about three-quarters full. Bake the cupcakes for 17 to 19 minutes, or until a cake tester or toothpick comes out clean from the centers. Let the cupcakes cool in the pan for 10 minutes, then transfer them to a cooling rack to finish cooling.

Make the cream cheese frosting while the cupcakes cool. Add the butter to a large bowl and whip it with an electric mixer on high speed for 5 to 10 minutes, until it is pale in color, fluffy and has doubled in size. Add the cream cheese and mix on medium-high speed until thoroughly combined.

Next, sift the powdered sugar into the mixture 1 cup (130 g) at a time. Mix on low, then medium, speed, making sure the first addition is fully combined before adding the last. When the last addition is incorporated, mix on high speed for about 1 minute, until the frosting is light and fluffy. Transfer the cream cheese frosting to a piping bag fitted with a decorative tip.

Once the cupcakes are completely cooled, pipe a generous amount of frosting onto each cupcake. Sprinkle extra pecans on top and serve!

Coconut Cream Pie Cupcakes

Traditionally, coconut cream pie comprises a flaky pie crust filled with a layer of coconut pastry cream and a layer of whipped cream. The old-fashioned dessert has been remade into cupcakes in this recipe! Soft and super moist coconut cupcakes are filled with a smooth and truly out-of-this-world coconut pastry cream. They're topped with a light coconut whipped cream frosting and sprinkled with toasted coconut for a finishing touch.

Yield: 12 cupcakes

For the Coconut Pastry Cream Filling
½ cup (120 ml) whole milk

2 egg yolks

6 tbsp (75 g) granulated sugar

Pinch of salt

¾ tsp vanilla bean paste or extract

¾ tsp coconut extract

2 tbsp (16 g) cornstarch, scooped and leveled

3 tbsp (18 g) shredded, sweetened coconut

For the Coconut Cupcakes
1¼ cups (140 g) cake flour, spooned and leveled

¾ tsp baking powder

⅛ tsp baking soda

¼ tsp salt

5 tbsp (70 g) unsalted butter, softened

¾ cup (150 g) granulated sugar

3 egg whites, at room temperature

1 tsp vanilla bean paste or extract

1 tsp coconut extract

¼ cup (61 g) sour cream, at room temperature

½ cup (120 ml) canned, full fat coconut milk

For the Coconut Whipped Cream Frosting
1 cup (240 ml) heavy whipping cream, cold

½ cup (65 g) powdered sugar

½ tsp coconut extract

Toasted coconut, for topping (optional)

Make the coconut pastry cream filling first so it has plenty of time to cool. In a small saucepan, heat the milk over medium-low heat just until it's steaming. Then turn the heat down to low until ready to use. To a separate small saucepan, with the heat off, add the egg yolks, sugar, salt, vanilla extract and coconut extract and whisk until combined and a pale-yellow color. It will be thick at first but will get smooth as you whisk. Gradually mix in the cornstarch 1 tablespoon (8 g) at a time, making sure each addition is fully combined before adding the next. When all the cornstarch is added, heat the mixture over medium-low heat. Whisk continuously for 2 to 3 minutes, until the sugar looks dissolved and the mixture is hot. Then turn the heat down to low.

To the mixture, add 2 tablespoons (30 ml) of the heated milk while stirring vigorously for 15 to 30 seconds until combined. Add the rest in and stir to combine. Increase the heat to medium-low again and cook for 1 to 2 minutes, whisking continually until the mixture is thick and soft peaks form. Remove the pastry cream from the heat. Transfer it to a bowl and mix in the shredded coconut. Place plastic wrap directly on top of the pastry cream to prevent a skin from forming. Chill it in the fridge until completely cold. Once the pastry cream is cold, transfer it to a piping bag until ready to use.

(continued)

Troubleshooting the pastry cream: If the pastry cream is too thick, add more heated milk 1 tablespoon (15 ml) at a time to thin it out slightly. If it starts to get lumpy after the milk is originally added, remove it from the heat and whisk vigorously to smooth out the lumps. Then return to heat and cook until thick.

To make the coconut cupcakes, preheat the oven to 350°F (177°C). Line a cupcake pan with 12 liners and set aside. In a small bowl, whisk together the cake flour, baking powder, baking soda and salt, then set aside. In a large bowl, cream the butter and granulated sugar together with an electric mixer on high speed for 2 to 3 minutes, until fluffy. Add the egg whites, vanilla and coconut extracts and mix on medium-high speed for 1 to 2 minutes, until pale and smooth. Scrape the sides and bottom of the bowl with a spatula as necessary. Pour in the sour cream and coconut milk and mix on medium speed just until combined.

Add the dry ingredients to the wet ingredients a little at a time until all has been added, mixing on low, then medium, speed for each addition. Mix just until the batter is combined and smooth, scraping the sides of the bowl as necessary.

Divide the batter evenly among the 12 liners until each is about three-quarters full. Bake the cupcakes for 17 to 19 minutes, or until a cake tester or toothpick comes out clean from the centers. Let the cupcakes cool in their pan for 10 minutes, then transfer them to a cooling rack to finish cooling.

Make the coconut whipped cream frosting when the cupcakes are completely cooled. Add the heavy cream to a large bowl. With an electric mixer, whip the cream on high for about 1 minute, until soft peaks form. Then sift in the powdered sugar and add the coconut extract. Whisk on high again for about 30 seconds until stiff peaks form. Cover the bowl with plastic wrap and place in the fridge until ready to use. Once ready to use, transfer the whipped cream to a piping bag fitted with a decorative tip.

Please see page 15 for instructions on how to assemble filled cupcakes, using the coconut pastry cream and whipped cream when indicated. Sprinkle toasted coconut (if using) over each, then serve!

Boston Cream Pie Mini Cake

Boston cream pie is no pie at all, but a cake! For this recipe, a mini, three-layer version of the classic is replicated. Moist and fluffy vanilla cake layers are filled with a glorious vanilla pastry cream that is good enough to eat with a spoon. The cake is finished with a thick and delicious semi-sweet chocolate ganache drip. This mini cake is easy to make, even easier to assemble, and just an absolute showstopper of a dessert!

Yield: 1 (4-inch [10-cm]) three-tier cake

For the Vanilla Pastry Cream
¾ cup (180 ml) milk

3 egg yolks

½ cup (100 g) granulated sugar

⅛ tsp salt

1 tsp vanilla extract

3 tbsp (24 g) cornstarch, scooped and leveled

¼ tsp salt

5 tbsp (70 g) unsalted butter, softened

¾ cup (150 g) granulated sugar

1 egg, at room temperature

1 egg yolk, at room temperature

1 tsp vanilla bean paste or extract

½ cup (120 ml) buttermilk, at room temperature

For the Vanilla Cake
1 cup + 2 tbsp (141 g) all-purpose flour, spooned and leveled

¾ tsp baking powder

⅛ tsp baking soda

For the Chocolate Ganache
2 tbsp (30 ml) heavy cream

¼ cup (42 g) semi-sweet chocolate chips

Make the vanilla pastry cream first so it has plenty of time to cool. In a small saucepan, heat the milk over medium-low heat just until it's steaming. Then turn the heat down to low until ready to use. To a separate small saucepan, with the heat off, add the egg yolks, sugar, salt and vanilla. Whisk until combined and a pale-yellow color. It will be thick at first but will get smooth as you whisk. Gradually sift in the cornstarch 1 tablespoon (8 g) at a time, making sure to fully whisk in each addition before adding the next. When all the cornstarch is added, heat the mixture over medium-low heat. Whisk continually for 2 to 3 minutes, until the sugar looks dissolved and the mixture is hot. Then turn the heat down to low.

To the mixture, pour in 3 tablespoons (45 ml) of the heated milk while stirring vigorously. Then add the rest and stir to combine. Increase the heat to medium-low and cook for 2 to 3 minutes, whisking continually until the mixture is thick and soft peaks form. Remove the pastry cream from heat. Transfer it to a bowl and place plastic wrap directly on top of the pastry cream to prevent a skin from forming. Chill it in the fridge until completely cold.

For tips on troubleshooting pastry cream, see page 68.

To make the vanilla cake, preheat the oven to 350°F (177°C). Spray three 4-inch (10-cm) cake pans with nonstick spray and line the bottoms with parchment paper rounds. In a small bowl, sift together the all-purpose flour, baking powder, baking soda and salt, then set aside. In a large bowl, cream the butter and granulated sugar together with an electric mixer on high speed for 2 to 3 minutes, until fluffy. Add the egg, egg yolk and vanilla and mix on medium-high speed for 1 to 2 minutes, or until the mixture is pale, smooth and slightly fluffy. Scrape the sides and bottom of the bowl with a spatula as necessary.

(continued)

Alternate adding the dry ingredients and the buttermilk to the butter mixture a little at a time until each has been added completely, mixing on low, then medium, speed for each addition. Mix just until the batter is combined and smooth, scraping the sides of the bowl as necessary.

Divide the batter evenly among the cake pans. Bake the cakes for 26 to 29 minutes, or until a cake tester or toothpick comes out clean from the centers. Let the cakes cool in their pans for 2 minutes, then transfer them to a cooling rack to finish cooling.

Make the chocolate ganache once the cake layers and the pastry cream are completely cooled. Add the cream to a small bowl and microwave it for 30 seconds or heat it on the stovetop in a very small saucepan until steaming, then transfer it to a small bowl. Add the chocolate chips and stir until the melted chocolate and cream are combined.

To assemble the Boston Cream Pie Mini Cake, you'll first want to make sure the cake layers are even and have a flat top so that they stack properly. With a sharp knife, cut each domed top off so that each layer is even. Then transfer the vanilla pastry cream to a piping bag fitted with a decorative tip. Transfer the ganache to a piping bag, but don't cut the tip off until ready to use. Place the first cake layer on whatever you plan to serve the cake on. Then pipe about half of the pastry cream onto the cake layer. I did decorative swirls so that it looked pretty, but you can also just pipe a large spiral of pastry cream if you would rather. Then place the second cake layer over the top and repeat the step. Place the final cake layer and then go around the top edges of the cake and squeeze the chocolate ganache so it starts to drip down the sides of the cake. Space your drips out about every quarter- to half-inch (6-mm to 1-cm). Also squeeze ganache on the top of the cake and smooth it out slightly with an offset spatula. As the ganache sits it will smooth out and come together to form a beautiful finish on top of the cake. Once set, cut and serve the cake!

Fruity Favorites

This sunny and colorful chapter will get you ready to usher in spring and summer, with lots of citrus and berries to be found among these fruit-forward creations. Full of zesty and bright flavors, in this section you'll find all the fruity flavor combinations imaginable. Try recipes like Orange Creamsicle Cupcakes (page 84), Strawberry Basil Cupcakes (page 76), Lemon Velvet Mini Cake (page 83) and Raspberry Lemonade Cupcakes (page 75). These fruity favorites are easy, breezy and delicious!

Raspberry Lemonade Cupcakes

These super fun cupcakes are literally raspberry lemonade in cupcake form! Soft and moist lemonade cupcakes are flavored with lemon zest and lemonade powder to really pack a lemony punch. After baking they're piped with a tangy raspberry lemonade frosting. Top with a paper straw for the cutest cupcakes ever.

Yield: 12 cupcakes

For the Lemonade Cupcakes

1 cup + 2 tbsp (141 g) all-purpose flour, spooned and leveled

¾ tsp baking powder

⅛ tsp baking soda

¼ tsp salt

5 tbsp (70 g) unsalted butter, softened

¾ cup (150 g) granulated sugar

2 egg whites, at room temperature

3 tbsp (39 g) lemonade powder, scooped and leveled (Country Time® was used)

2 tsp (2 g) lemon zest

½ cup (120 ml) buttermilk, at room temperature

1–2 drops yellow food coloring (optional)

For the Raspberry Lemonade Cream Cheese Frosting

3 tbsp (39 g) lemonade powder, scooped and leveled

2 tsp (10 ml) water

¾ cup (18 g) whole freeze-dried raspberries

½ cup (112 g) unsalted butter, softened

4 oz (114 g) cream cheese, cold

2½ cups (325 g) powdered sugar

12 lemon slices, for decoration (optional)

12 raspberries, for decoration (optional)

Trimmed paper straws, for decoration (optional)

To make the lemonade cupcakes, preheat the oven to 350°F (177°C). Line a cupcake pan with 12 liners and set aside. In a small bowl, sift together the flour, baking powder, baking soda and salt, then set aside. In a large bowl, cream the butter and granulated sugar together with an electric mixer on high speed for 2 to 3 minutes, until it is light and fluffy. Next, add in the egg whites and mix on medium-high speed for 1 to 2 minutes, until pale and smooth. Add the lemonade powder and lemon zest and mix on medium speed just until combined. Alternate adding the dry ingredients and the buttermilk to the butter mixture a little at a time until each has been added completely, mixing on low, then medium, for each addition. Mix just until the batter is combined and smooth. Add the yellow food coloring (if using) and mix on medium-low speed just until combined.

Divide the batter evenly among the 12 liners until each is two-thirds to three-quarters full. Bake the cupcakes for 17 to 20 minutes, or until a cake tester or toothpick comes out clean from the centers. Let the cupcakes cool in the pan for 10 minutes, then transfer them to a cooling rack.

To make the raspberry lemonade cream cheese frosting, add the lemonade powder and water to a small bowl. Microwave it for 25 to 35 seconds or until the lemonade is dissolved. Then let it cool completely.

Place the freeze-dried raspberries in a baggie. Crush the raspberries using a rolling pin until they are very finely ground. Keep the raspberries in the bag until ready to add to the frosting. Add the butter to a large bowl. Whip it with an electric mixer on high speed for 5 to 10 minutes, until the butter is pale, fluffy and doubled in size. Add the cream cheese and mix on medium-high speed until it is thoroughly combined. Sift the powdered sugar into the mixture 1 cup (130 g) at a time. Mix on low, then medium, speed, making sure the first addition is fully combined before adding the next. Add the freeze-dried raspberry powder and mix on medium-low speed until combined. Add the cooled lemonade mixture and mix on medium, then high, speed for about 1 minute, until the frosting is light and fluffy. Transfer the frosting to a piping bag fitted with a decorative tip.

Once the cupcakes are cooled, pipe a generous amount of frosting onto each. Top with a lemon slice, raspberry, and a paper straw (if using), then serve!

Strawberry Basil Cupcakes

If you've never tried the strawberry and basil flavor combination, you are in for a treat! Strawberry and basil just work so well together because basil adds a nice balance of brightness to sweet strawberries. These strawberry basil cupcakes are made with a fresh strawberry reduction to add all the strawberry flavor without the excess moisture. Fresh, finely chopped basil gets mixed right into the batter, and after baking the cupcakes are piped with a delightful strawberry basil cream cheese frosting.

Yield: 12 cupcakes

For the Strawberry Reduction
8 oz (226 g) fresh strawberries, hulled

For the Strawberry Basil Cupcakes
1¼ cups (140 g) cake flour, spooned and leveled

¾ tsp baking powder

⅛ tsp baking soda

¼ tsp salt

5 tbsp (70 g) unsalted butter, softened

¾ cup (150 g) granulated sugar

3 egg whites, at room temperature

1 tsp vanilla bean paste or extract

2 tsp (2 g) finely chopped fresh basil

⅓ cup (80 ml) buttermilk, at room temperature

For the Strawberry Basil Cream Cheese Frosting
½ cup (112 g) unsalted butter, softened

4 oz (114 g) cream cheese, cold

2½ cups (325 g) powdered sugar

¾ cup (15 g) freeze-dried strawberries

2 tsp (2 g) finely chopped basil

12 strawberry slices, for decoration (optional)

12 basil leaves, for decoration (optional)

Start the strawberry reduction so it has plenty of time to cool. Add the strawberries to a blender or food processor and blend until puréed. Transfer to a large saucepan. Heat the strawberry purée over medium-low heat for 20 to 25 minutes, stirring occasionally, until it has reduced all the way down to ¼ cup (60 ml). Remove it from the heat and allow it to cool completely.

To make the strawberry basil cupcakes, preheat oven to 350°F (177°C). Line a cupcake pan with 12 liners and set aside. In a small bowl, whisk together the cake flour, baking powder, baking soda and salt, then set aside. In a large bowl, cream the butter and sugar together with an electric mixer on high speed for 2 to 3 minutes, until fluffy. Add the egg whites and vanilla and mix on medium-high speed for 1 to 2 minutes, until smooth and pale. Add the strawberry reduction and finely chopped basil and mix on medium speed just until combined. Alternate adding the dry ingredients and the buttermilk to the strawberry mixture a little at a time, until each has been added completely, mixing on low, then medium, speed for each addition. Mix just until the batter is combined and smooth. Divide the batter among the 12 liners until each is two-thirds to three-quarters full. Bake the cupcakes for 17 to 19 minutes, or until a cake tester or toothpick comes out clean from the centers. Let the cupcakes cool in the pan for 10 minutes, then transfer them to a cooling rack to finish cooling.

To make the strawberry basil cream cheese frosting, add the butter to a large bowl. Whip it with an electric mixer on high speed for 5 to 10 minutes, until the butter is pale, fluffy and doubled in size. Add the cream cheese and mix on medium-high speed until it is thoroughly combined. Sift the powdered sugar into the mixture about 1 cup (130 g) at a time. Mix on low, then medium, speed, making sure the first addition is fully combined before adding the next. Right before using, grind the freeze-dried strawberries in a food processor until very finely ground. Add them to the frosting and mix on medium-low speed until combined. Add the finely chopped basil and mix on medium, then high, speed for about 1 minute, until the frosting is light and fluffy. Transfer the frosting to a piping bag fitted with a decorative tip.

When the cupcakes are completely cooled, pipe a generous amount of frosting onto each cupcake and top with a strawberry slice and basil leaf (if using), then serve!

Roasted Strawberries & Cream Mini Cake

This is the grown-up version of strawberries and cream! Fresh strawberries are tossed with vanilla and sugar and are roasted until tender and perfectly juicy. The roasted strawberries are sandwiched between layers of moist and fluffy vanilla cake, all sealed together with luscious, silky-smooth cream cheese frosting. The cake is finished with a topping of extra roasted strawberries. Once you've tried roasted strawberries you won't want to have them prepared any other way!

Yield: 1 (4-inch [10-cm]) three-tier cake

For the Roasted Strawberries

18 oz (510 g) fresh strawberries, hulled and diced

6 tbsp (75 g) granulated sugar

1½ tsp (8 ml) vanilla bean paste or extract

For the Vanilla Cake

1 cup + 2 tbsp (141 g) all-purpose flour, spooned and leveled

¾ tsp baking powder

⅛ tsp baking soda

¼ tsp salt

5 tbsp (70 g) unsalted butter, softened

¾ cup (150 g) granulated sugar

1 egg, at room temperature

1 egg yolk, at room temperature

1 tsp vanilla bean paste or extract

½ cup (120 ml) buttermilk, at room temperature

For the Cream Cheese Frosting

½ cup (112 g) unsalted butter, softened

4 oz (114 g) cream cheese, cold

2½ cups (325 g) powdered sugar

Make the roasted strawberries first so they have plenty of time to cool. Preheat the oven to 350°F (177°C). Add the diced strawberries, sugar and vanilla to a medium-sized bowl. Stir to combine, then spread out on a parchment paper–lined baking sheet. Bake the strawberries for 45 minutes, stirring every 15 minutes. After baking, transfer the strawberries and thickened juice to a bowl to cool completely.

To make the vanilla cake, preheat the oven to 350°F (177 °C). Spray three 4-inch (10-cm) cake pans with nonstick spray and line the bottoms with parchment paper rounds, then set aside. In a small bowl, sift together the all-purpose flour, baking powder, baking soda and salt, then set aside. In a large bowl, cream the butter and granulated sugar together with an electric mixer on high speed for 2 to 3 minutes, until fluffy. Add the egg, egg yolk and vanilla and mix on medium-high speed for 1 to 2 minutes, or until the mixture is pale, smooth and slightly fluffy. Scrape the sides and bottom of the bowl with a spatula as necessary.

Alternate adding the dry ingredients and the buttermilk to the butter mixture a little at a time, until each has been added completely, mixing on low, then medium, speed for each addition. Mix just until the batter is combined and smooth, scraping the sides of the bowl as necessary. Divide the batter evenly among the cake pans. Bake the cakes for 24 to 28 minutes, or until a cake tester or toothpick comes out clean from the centers. Let the cakes cool in their pans for 2 minutes, then transfer them to a cooling rack to finish cooling.

Make the cream cheese frosting while waiting for the cakes to cool. Add the butter to a large bowl. Whip it with an electric mixer on high speed for 5 to 10 minutes, until the butter is pale, fluffy, and doubled in size. Add the cream cheese and mix on medium-high speed until thoroughly combined. Sift the powdered sugar into the mixture about 1 cup (130 g) at a time. Mix on low, then medium, speed, making sure the first addition is fully combined before adding the next. When the last addition is added, mix on high speed for about 1 minute, until the frosting is light and fluffy.

Please see page 12 for mini cake assembly instructions, using the roasted strawberries as filling and topping and the cream cheese frosting when indicated, then serve and enjoy!

Blueberries & Cream Cupcakes

Peaches and cream and strawberries and cream are both things, but blueberries and cream? Trust me, you will love this combo! These soft and fluffy white cupcakes are filled with a blueberry jam and topped with swirls of absolutely delicious blueberry cream cheese frosting. One bite and you'll be wondering why you hadn't tried this combination sooner!

Yield: 12 cupcakes

For the Blueberry Jam
12 oz (340 g) fresh blueberries
½ cup (100 g) granulated sugar
1 tsp vanilla bean paste or extract

For the White Cupcakes
1¼ cups (140 g) cake flour, spooned and leveled
¾ tsp baking powder
⅛ tsp baking soda
¼ tsp salt

5 tbsp (70 g) unsalted butter, softened
¾ cup (150 g) granulated sugar
2 egg whites, room temperature
1½ tsp (8 ml) vanilla extract
½ cup (120 ml) buttermilk, at room temperature

For the Blueberry Cream Cheese Frosting
½ cup (112 g) unsalted butter, softened
4 oz (114 g) cream cheese, cold
2 cups (260 g) powdered sugar

Start the blueberry jam first so it has plenty of time to cool. Add the blueberries to a blender and blend until they are puréed. Add the purée to a large saucepan. Stir in the sugar and vanilla. Heat over medium-low heat, stirring occasionally, until the purée has thickened into a jam-like consistency and measures out to ¾ cup (180 ml). This will take 15 to 20 minutes. Remove the jam the heat and allow it to cool completely.

To make the white cupcakes, preheat the oven to 350°F (177°C). Line a cupcake pan with 12 liners and set aside. In a small bowl, sift together the cake flour, baking powder, baking soda and salt, then set aside. In a large bowl, cream the butter and sugar together with an electric mixer on high speed for 2 to 3 minutes, until it is light and fluffy. Add the egg whites and vanilla and mix on medium-high speed for 1 to 2 minutes, until pale and smooth. Alternate adding the dry ingredients and the buttermilk to the butter mixture a little at a time until each has been added completely, mixing on low, then medium, speed for each addition. Mix just until the batter is combined and smooth, scraping the sides of the bowl with a spatula as necessary. The batter will be thick.

Divide the batter evenly among the 12 liners until each is two-thirds to three-quarters full. Bake the cupcakes for 16 to 18 minutes, or until a cake tester or toothpick comes out clean from the centers. Let the cupcakes cool in the pan for 10 minutes, then transfer them to a cooling rack to finish cooling.

To make the blueberry cream cheese frosting, add the butter to a large bowl. Whip it with an electric mixer on high speed for 5 to 10 minutes, until the butter is pale, fluffy and doubled in size. Add the cream cheese and mix on medium-high speed until thoroughly combined. Next, sift the powdered sugar into the mixture 1 cup (130 g) at a time. Mix on low, then medium, speed, making sure the first addition is fully combined before adding the last.

When the last addition is incorporated, add 2 tablespoons (30 ml) of blueberry jam and mix on medium, then high, speed for about 1 minute, until the frosting is light and fluffy. Transfer the frosting to a piping bag fitted with a decorative tip.

Please see page 15 for filled cupcake assembly instructions, using the blueberry jam as filling and blueberry cream cheese frosting when indicated, then serve and enjoy!

Lemon Velvet Mini Cake

I'm calling this lemon velvet cake because it has the most incredible velvety texture. It's extremely moist due to the buttermilk and has the most perfect zesty lemon flavor, achieved with lemon zest and lemon extract. It's frosted with a creamy and delicious lemon cream cheese frosting, which is quite literally the icing on the cake. This bright cake is simple yet absolutely delectable, and sure to be a new classic. This recipe is dedicated to Kori, who asked me to make her the best lemon cake imaginable.

Yield: 1 (4-inch [10-cm]) three-tier cake

For the Lemon Cake	For the Lemon Cream Cheese Frosting
1¼ cups (140 g) cake flour, spooned and leveled	½ cup (112 g) unsalted butter, softened
¾ tsp baking powder	4 oz (114 g) cream cheese, cold
⅛ tsp baking soda	2½ cups (325 g) sifted powdered sugar
¼ tsp salt	1 tsp lemon extract
5 tbsp (70 g) unsalted butter, softened	1 tsp lemon zest
¾ cup (150 g) granulated sugar	2–4 drops yellow food coloring (optional)
2 egg whites, at room temperature	
1 tbsp (4 g) lemon zest	Lemon zest, for decoration (optional)
1 tsp lemon extract	Lemon peel, for decoration (optional)
½ cup (120 ml) buttermilk, at room temperature	
2–4 drops yellow food coloring (optional)	

To make the lemon cake, preheat the oven to 350°F (177°C). Spray three 4-inch (10-cm) cake pans with nonstick spray. In a small bowl, sift together the cake flour, baking powder, baking soda and salt, then set aside. In a large bowl, cream the butter and sugar together with an electric mixer on high speed for 2 to 3 minutes, until fluffy. Add the egg whites and mix on high speed for 2 to 3 minutes, until the mixture is pale and fluffy. Scrape the sides and bottom of the bowl with a spatula as necessary.

Next, add the lemon zest and lemon extract and mix on medium speed just until combined. Alternate adding the dry ingredients and the buttermilk to the butter mixture a little at a time until each has been added completely, mixing on low, then medium, speed for each addition. Mix just until the batter is combined and smooth, scraping the sides and bottom of the bowl with a spatula as necessary. Add 2 to 4 drops of yellow food coloring if you desire the cake to have a yellow hue.

Divide the batter evenly among the cake pans. Bake the cakes for 25 to 30 minutes, or until a cake tester or toothpick comes out clean from the centers. Let the cakes cool in their pans for 2 minutes, then transfer them to a cooling rack to finish cooling.

To make the lemon cream cheese frosting, add the butter to a large bowl. Whip it with an electric mixer for 5 to 10 minutes, until the butter is pale, fluffy and doubled in size. Add the cream cheese and mix on medium-high speed until it is thoroughly combined. Sift the powdered sugar into the mixture about 1 cup (130 g) at a time. Mix on low, then medium, speed, making sure the first addition is fully combined before adding the next. When the last addition is incorporated, add the lemon extract, lemon zest and yellow food coloring (if using) and mix on medium, then high, speed for about 1 minute, until the frosting is light and fluffy.

Please see page 12 for mini cake assembly instructions, using the lemon cream cheese frosting when indicated. Decorate with lemon zest and lemon peel (if using), then serve!

Orange Creamsicle Cupcakes

Just like the creamy orange popsicles from childhood, these Orange Creamsicle Cupcakes are packed full of bright and refreshing orange flavor. They're super soft and tender, flavored with orange zest, juice and extract to produce the best orange essence. They're topped with a super creamy orange cream cheese frosting and an orange slice for maximum cuteness!

Yield: 12 cupcakes

For the Orange Cupcakes

1 cup + 2 tbsp (141 g) all-purpose flour, spooned and leveled

¾ tsp baking powder

⅛ tsp baking soda

¼ tsp salt

5 tbsp (70 g) unsalted butter, softened

¾ cup (150 g) granulated sugar

1 egg, at room temperature

1 egg yolk, at room temperature

1½ tsp vanilla bean paste or extract

1 tsp orange extract

¼ cup (60 ml) buttermilk, at room temperature

¼ cup (60 ml) orange juice, at room temperature

1 tsp orange zest

1–2 drops orange food coloring (optional)

For the Orange Cream Cheese Frosting

½ cup (112 g) unsalted butter, softened

4 oz (114 g) cream cheese, cold

2 cups (260 g) powdered sugar

1 tsp orange extract

1 tsp orange zest

1–2 drops orange food coloring (optional)

12 orange slices, for decoration (optional)

To make the orange cupcakes, preheat the oven to 350°F (177°C). Line a cupcake pan with 12 liners and set aside. In a small bowl, sift together the flour, baking powder, baking soda and salt, then set aside. In a large bowl, cream the butter and sugar together with an electric mixer on high speed for 2 to 3 minutes, until it is light and fluffy. Add the egg, egg yolk, vanilla and orange extract and mix on medium-high speed for 1 to 2 minutes, until pale, smooth and slightly fluffy. Scrape the sides and bottom of the bowl with a spatula as necessary.

Add half the dry ingredients and the buttermilk to the butter mixture and mix on low, then medium, speed until combined. Add the orange juice and the rest of the dry ingredients and mix on low, then medium, speed until the batter is smooth. Add the orange zest and orange food coloring (if using) and mix on medium-low speed just until combined.

Divide the batter evenly among the 12 liners until each is two-thirds to three-quarters full. Bake the cupcakes for 16 to 19 minutes, or until a cake tester or toothpick comes out clean from the centers. Let the cupcakes cool in the pan for 10 minutes, then transfer them to a cooling rack to finish cooling.

Make the orange cream cheese frosting while the cupcakes cool. Add the butter to a large bowl and whip it with an electric mixer for 5 to 10 minutes, until it is pale, fluffy and has doubled in size. Add the cream cheese and mix on medium-high speed until thoroughly combined. Next, sift the powdered sugar into the mixture 1 cup (130 g) at a time. Mix on low, then medium, speed, making sure the first addition is fully combined before adding the last. When the last addition is incorporated, add the orange extract, orange zest and orange food coloring (if using) and mix on medium, then high, speed for about 1 minute, until the frosting is light and fluffy. Transfer the frosting to a piping bag fitted with a decorative tip.

Once the cupcakes are completely cooled, pipe a generous amount of orange cream cheese frosting onto each cupcake and top with an orange slice (if using), then serve!

Coconut Raspberry Swirl Cupcakes

These cupcakes are pretty, pink and so delicious! Pillowy soft coconut cupcakes are coupled with a swirl of homemade raspberry jam and topped with a generous piping of luscious coconut raspberry cream cheese frosting. These sweet and bright cupcakes are sure to delight your tastebuds in the most exciting way!

Yield: 12 cupcakes

For the Raspberry Jam
12 oz (340 g) fresh raspberries
¾ cup (150 g) granulated sugar
1 tsp vanilla bean paste or extract

For the Coconut Cupcakes
1¼ cups (140 g) cake flour, spooned and leveled
¾ tsp baking powder
⅛ tsp baking soda
¼ tsp salt
5 tbsp (70 g) unsalted butter, softened
¾ cup (150 g) granulated sugar
3 egg whites, at room temperature

1 tsp vanilla bean paste or extract
1 tsp coconut extract
¼ cup (61 g) sour cream, at room temperature
½ cup (120 ml) canned, full fat coconut milk

For the Coconut Raspberry Cream Cheese Frosting
½ cup (112 g) unsalted butter, softened
4 oz (114 g) cream cheese, cold
2 cups (260 g) powdered sugar
1 tsp coconut extract
12 raspberries, for decoration (optional)
Shredded coconut, for decoration (optional)

Start the raspberry jam first so it has plenty of time to cool. Add the raspberries to a blender and blend until they are puréed. Strain the berries over a large saucepan to separate most of the seeds from the purée. Add the sugar and vanilla. Heat over medium heat for 15 to 20 minutes, stirring occasionally, until the purée has thickened into a jammy consistency and measures out to ¾ cup (180 ml). Remove the jam from the heat and allow it to cool completely. Once cooled, measure out 2 tablespoons (30 ml) to use in the cupcake batter and set aside.

To make the cupcakes, preheat the oven to 350°F (177°C). Line a cupcake pan with 12 liners. In a small bowl, sift together the cake flour, baking powder, baking soda and salt, then set aside. In a large bowl, cream the butter and granulated sugar together with an electric mixer on high speed for 2 to 3 minutes, until fluffy. Add the egg whites, vanilla and coconut extract and mix on medium-high speed for 1 to 2 minutes, until pale and smooth. Then add the sour cream and coconut milk and mix on medium speed just until combined. Add the dry ingredients to the wet ingredients a little at a time until all has been added, mixing on low, then medium, speed for each addition. Mix just until the batter is combined and smooth. Divide the batter evenly among the 12 liners until each is about three-quarters full. Add one heaping teaspoon of jam to each batter-filled liner. With a butter knife, swirl the jam into the batter without mixing it in completely. Bake the cupcakes for 18 to 22 minutes, or until a cake tester or toothpick comes out clean from the centers. Let the cupcakes cool in the pan for 10 minutes, then transfer them to a cooling rack to finish cooling.

To make the coconut raspberry cream cheese frosting, add the butter to a large bowl. Whip it with an electric mixer on high speed for 10 to 15 minutes, until the butter is pale, fluffy and doubled in size. Add the cream cheese and mix on medium-high speed until thoroughly combined. Next, sift the powdered sugar into the mixture 1 cup (130 g) at a time. Mix on low, then medium, speed, making sure the first addition is fully combined before adding the next. When the last addition is incorporated, add the coconut extract and 2 tablespoons (30 ml) of raspberry jam and mix on medium, then high, speed for about 1 minute, until the frosting is light and fluffy. Transfer the frosting to a piping bag fitted with a decorative tip.

Once the cupcakes are cooled, pipe a generous amount of frosting onto each and top with a raspberry and shredded coconut (if using), then serve!

Lemon Basil Blueberry Jam Mini Cake

This cake just absolutely screams summer! Layers of moist and tender lemon cake are speckled with fresh, finely chopped basil, filled with homemade blueberry jam and frosted with blueberry lemon buttercream. This fruity little cake is sure to be a showstopper at any summer get-together.

Yield: 1 (4-inch [10-cm]) three-tier cake

For the Blueberry Jam
12 oz (340 g) fresh blueberries

½ cup (100 g) granulated sugar

2 tsp (10 ml) fresh lemon juice

For the Lemon Basil Cake
1 cup + 2 tbsp (141 g) all-purpose flour, spooned and leveled

¾ tsp baking powder

⅛ tsp baking soda

¼ tsp salt

5 tbsp (70 g) unsalted butter, softened

¾ cup (150 g) granulated sugar

1 egg, at room temperature

1 egg yolk, at room temperature

½ cup (120 ml) buttermilk, at room temperature

1 tbsp (6 g) lemon zest

1 tbsp (3 g) fresh basil, finely chopped

For the Blueberry Lemon Buttercream
¾ cup (168 g) unsalted butter, softened

⅛ tsp salt

2 cups (260 g) powdered sugar

1 tsp lemon zest

Blueberries, for decoration (optional)

Lemon slices, for decoration (optional)

Basil leaves, for decoration (optional)

Start the blueberry jam first. Add the blueberries to a blender and blend until they are puréed. Add the blueberry purée, sugar and lemon juice to a large pot. Stir to combine. Heat over medium-low heat, stirring occasionally until the purée has thickened into a jam-like consistency and measures out to ¾ cup (180 ml). This will take 15 to 20 minutes. Remove the jam from the heat and allow it to cool completely.

To make the lemon basil cake, preheat the oven to 350°F (177°C). Spray three 4-inch (10-cm) cake pans with nonstick spray. In a small bowl, sift together the flour, baking powder, baking soda and salt, then set aside. In a large bowl, cream the butter and granulated sugar together with an electric mixer on high speed for 2 to 3 minutes, until fluffy. Add the egg and egg yolk and mix on medium-high speed for 1 to 2 minutes, or until the mixture is pale, smooth and slightly fluffy. Alternate adding the dry ingredients and the buttermilk to the butter mixture a little at a time, until each has been added completely, mixing on low then medium speed for each addition. Mix just until the batter is combined and smooth. Lastly, add in the lemon zest and finely chopped basil and mix on low speed just until they are dispersed through the batter. The batter will be thick.

Divide the batter evenly among the cake pans. Bake the cakes for 25 to 28 minutes, or until a cake tester or toothpick comes out clean from the centers. Let the cakes cool in their pans for 2 minutes, then transfer them to a cooling rack to finish cooling.

To make the blueberry lemon buttercream, add the butter and salt to a large bowl. Whip it with an electric mixer on high speed for 5 to 10 minutes, until the butter is pale, fluffy, and doubled in size. Sift the powdered sugar into the mixture 1 cup (130 g) at a time. Mix on low, then medium, speed, making sure the first addition is fully combined before adding the last. Next, add 2 tablespoons (30 ml) of blueberry jam and the lemon zest and mix on medium speed until combined. Mix the frosting on high speed for about 1 minute, until it is light and fluffy.

Please see page 12 for how to assemble mini cakes, using the blueberry jam as filling and blueberry lemon frosting when indicated. Decorate with blueberries, a lemon slice and basil leaves (if using), then serve.

Salted Caramel Banana Bread Mini Cake

Banana bread is one of my all-time favorite things to bake, so I turned it into a cake! It also turns out that adding salted caramel sauce to banana bread is the absolute best move. Here, homemade salted caramel sauce is used to make the best salted caramel buttercream, which is layered between super moist banana bread cake layers. The cake is frosted with more salted caramel buttercream and finished with a beautiful salted caramel drip and buttercream swirls. Add banana slices for an extra special touch!

Yield: 1 (4-inch [10-cm]) three-tier cake

For the Salted Caramel Sauce
½ cup (100 g) granulated sugar

3 tbsp (42 g) unsalted butter, softened

¼ cup (60 ml) heavy cream, at room temperature

⅛–¼ tsp salt (depending on preference)

½ tsp vanilla bean paste or extract

For the Banana Bread Cake
1 cup + 2 tbsp (141 g) all-purpose flour, spooned and leveled

¾ tsp baking powder

⅛ tsp baking soda

¼ tsp salt

5 tbsp (70 g) unsalted butter, softened

¾ cup (150 g) granulated sugar

1 egg, at room temperature

1 egg yolk, at room temperature

1 tsp vanilla bean paste or extract

½ cup (125 g) mashed banana

¼ cup (60 ml) buttermilk, at room temperature

For the Salted Caramel Buttercream
¾ cup unsalted butter, softened

⅛ tsp salt

1½ cups (195 g) powdered sugar

Banana slices, for decoration

Make the salted caramel sauce first so it has plenty of time to cool. Add the granulated sugar to a small saucepan and heat it over medium-low heat. As the sugar is heating it will crystalize and then eventually all melt down and turn golden in color. When most of the sugar has melted, but there are still a few crystalized clumps, turn the heat down to low so the melted sugar doesn't burn. Melting all the sugar should take 10 to 15 minutes.

Once all the sugar has melted and turned golden in color, add the butter right away. Stir quickly until the butter is incorporated. Then add the heavy cream and stir quickly again to incorporate everything. At this point, if you see the butter and cream start to separate from the sugar, turn up the heat to medium-low and stir vigorously to combine everything. Add the salt and vanilla and stir to combine. Let the caramel simmer for 1 to 2 minutes to allow it to thicken a little more. Remove the caramel from the heat and allow it to cool completely. Once cooled, measure out ¼ cup (70 g) to use in the frosting. Transfer the rest of the caramel to a piping bag to be used later on top of the cake.

(continued)

To make the banana bread cake, preheat the oven to 350°F (177°C). Spray three 4-inch (10-cm) cake pans with nonstick spray and line the bottoms with parchment paper rounds.

In a small bowl, sift together the flour, baking powder, baking soda and salt, then set aside. In a large bowl, cream the butter and granulated sugar together with an electric mixer on high speed for 2 to 3 minutes, until it is light and fluffy. Add the egg, egg yolk and vanilla and mix on medium-high speed for 1 to 2 minutes, until pale, smooth and slightly fluffy. Scrape the sides and bottom of the bowl with a spatula as necessary. Then add the mashed banana and mix on medium speed until combined. Alternate adding the dry ingredients and the buttermilk to the banana mixture a little at a time, until each has been added completely, mixing on low, then medium, speed for each addition. Mix just until the batter is combined, scraping the sides and bottom of the bowl as necessary.

Divide the batter evenly among the cake pans. Bake the cakes for 27 to 30 minutes, or until a cake tester or toothpick comes out clean from the centers. Let the cakes cool in their pans for 2 minutes, then transfer them to a cooling rack to finish cooling.

To make the salted caramel buttercream, add the butter and salt to a large bowl. Whip it with an electric mixer on high speed for 5 to 10 minutes, until the butter is pale, fluffy, and doubled in size. Add ¼ cup (70 g) of salted caramel sauce and combine on medium speed. Next, sift the powdered sugar into the mixture ½ cup (65 g) at a time. Mix on low, then medium, speed, making sure each addition is fully combined before adding the next. Scrape the sides and bottom of the bowl as necessary. When the last addition is added, mix on high speed for about 1 minute, until the frosting is light and fluffy.

Please see page 12 for mini cake assembly instructions, using the salted caramel buttercream and salted caramel sauce as a drip when indicated. Decorate with banana slices, then serve!

Lavender Blackberry Swirl Cupcakes

These cupcakes are the epitome of spring in a dessert. Tender lavender cupcakes are paired with a swirl of homemade blackberry jam and frosted with a smooth blackberry lavender cream cheese frosting. Decorate them with a blackberry and sprig of lavender for an extra elegant touch. Each bite is full of delicious jammy goodness that will leave you wanting more!

Yield: 12 cupcakes

For the Blackberry Jam

12 oz (340 g) fresh blackberries

½ cup (100 g) granulated sugar

1 tsp lemon juice

For the Lavender Blackberry Swirl Cupcakes

1¼ cups (140 g) cake flour, spooned and leveled

¾ tsp baking powder

⅛ tsp baking soda

¼ tsp salt

5 tbsp (70 g) unsalted butter, softened

¾ cup (150 g) granulated sugar

2 egg whites, at room temperature

1½ tsp (8 ml) lavender extract

½ cup (120 ml) buttermilk, at room temperature

For the Blackberry Lavender Cream Cheese Frosting

½ cup (112 g) unsalted butter, softened

4 oz (114 g) cream cheese, cold

2 cups (260 g) powdered sugar

1 tsp lavender extract

12 blackberries, for decoration (optional)

12 lavender sprigs, for decoration (optional)

Start the blackberry jam first so it has plenty of time to cool. Add the blackberries to a blender and blend until they are puréed. Strain the purée over a large saucepan to separate most of the seeds from the purée. (It's okay if some get through. Additionally, this step is optional if you don't mind all the seeds). Add the sugar and lemon juice and mix to combine. Heat over medium heat for 15 to 20 minutes, stirring occasionally, until the purée has thickened into a jam-like consistency and measures out to ¾ cup (180 ml). Remove the jam from the heat and allow it to cool completely. Once cooled, measure out 2 tablespoons (30 ml) to use in the cake batter and set aside.

To make the lavender blackberry swirl cupcakes, preheat the oven to 350°F (177°C). Line a cupcake pan with 12 liners and set aside. In a small bowl, sift together the cake flour, baking powder, baking soda and salt, then set aside. In a large bowl, cream the butter and sugar together with an electric mixer on high speed for 2 to 3 minutes, until it is light and fluffy. Next, add the egg whites and lavender extract and mix on medium-high speed until pale and smooth. Scrape the sides and bottom of the bowl with a spatula as necessary. Alternate adding the dry ingredients and the buttermilk to the butter mixture a little at a time until each has been added completely, mixing on low, then medium, speed for each addition. Mix just until the batter is combined and smooth, scraping the sides and bottom of the bowl as necessary.

(continued)

Divide the batter evenly among the 12 cupcake liners until each is two-thirds to three-quarters full. Spoon a heaping teaspoon of blackberry jam into each batter-filled liner and gently swirl the jam with a butter knife, being careful not to mix it in completely. Bake the cupcakes for 18 to 21 minutes, or until a cake tester or toothpick comes out clean from the centers. Let the cupcakes cool in the pan for 10 minutes, then transfer them to a cooling rack to finish cooling.

To make the blackberry lavender cream cheese frosting, add the butter to a large bowl. Whip it with an electric mixer on high speed for 5 to 10 minutes, until the butter is pale, fluffy and doubled in size. Add the cream cheese and mix on medium-high speed until it is thoroughly combined. Sift the powdered sugar into the mixture 1 cup (130 g) at a time. Mix on low, then medium, speed, making sure the first addition is fully combined before adding the last. When the last addition is incorporated, add the lavender extract and 2 tablespoons (30 ml) of blackberry jam. Mix on medium, then high, speed for about 1 minute, until the frosting is light and fluffy. Transfer the frosting to a piping bag fitted with a decorative tip.

Once the cupcakes are cooled, pipe a generous amount of blackberry lavender frosting onto each. Top with a blackberry and lavender sprig (if using) and serve!

Contemporary Creations

This chapter is extra fun because it's a reflection of desserts and flavors that are newer to hit the scene but are sure to be here for the long run. Here you'll find some of the best dessert flavors this generation has offered us. Try the Cosmic Brownie Cupcakes (page 121), Salted Caramel Latte Mini Cake (page 100), Oreo® Cookie Butter Cupcakes (page 99) or Chocolate Chip Cookie Dough Mini Cake (page 109). These trendy flavor concepts will inspire your creativity and delight your tastebuds.

Oreo® Cookie Butter Cupcakes

Really, I'm not sure why I didn't think to put the world's best cookies, Lotus Biscoff® and Oreos, together sooner! These cupcakes have Biscoff cookie butter mixed right into the batter with crushed pieces of Oreos. They're topped with a truly decadent cookie butter and Oreo buttercream and finished with crushed Lotus Biscoff and Oreo pieces. Garnish with half an Oreo and half a Biscoff cookie for an ultimate "wow" factor!

Yield: 12 cupcakes

For the Oreo® Cookie Butter Cupcakes
1 cup + 2 tbsp (141 g) all-purpose flour, spooned and leveled

¾ tsp baking powder

⅛ tsp baking soda

¼ tsp salt

¼ cup (56 g) unsalted butter, softened

¾ cup (150 g) granulated sugar

1 egg, at room temperature

1 egg yolk, at room temperature

1 tsp vanilla bean paste or extract

¼ cup (60 g) cookie butter (I used Biscoff)

½ cup (120 ml) buttermilk, at room temperature

5 Oreos, filling removed and crushed to small bits

For the Oreo® Cookie Butter Buttercream
¾ cup (168 g) unsalted butter, softened

⅛ tsp salt

¼ cup + 2 tbsp (90 g) cookie butter

1½ cups (195 g) powdered sugar

½ tsp vanilla bean paste or extract

5 Oreos, filling removed and finely ground

6 Oreos and 6 Lotus Biscoff cookies, halved with crumbs reserved for decoration (optional)

To make the Oreo® cookie butter cupcakes, start by preheating the oven to 350°F (177°C). Line a cupcake pan with 12 liners. In a small bowl, sift together the all-purpose flour, baking powder, baking soda and salt, then set aside. Add the butter and granulated sugar to a large bowl and cream together with an electric mixer on high speed for 2 to 3 minutes, until it is fluffy. Add the egg, egg yolk and vanilla and mix on medium-high speed for 1 to 2 minutes, until pale, smooth and slightly fluffy. Scrape the sides and bottom of the bowl with a spatula as necessary. Then add the cookie butter and mix on medium speed just until combined.

Add the dry ingredients and the buttermilk to the butter mixture a little at a time until it is all added, mixing on low, then medium, speed for each addition. Mix just until the batter is combined and smooth, scraping the sides and bottom of the bowl as necessary. Fold in the crushed Oreos.

Divide the batter evenly among the 12 cupcake liners until each is about three-quarters full. Bake the cupcakes for 18 to 22 minutes, or until a cake tester or toothpick comes out clean from the centers. Let the cupcakes cool in the pan for 10 minutes, then transfer them to a cooling rack to finish cooling.

To make the Oreo® cookie buttercream, add the butter and salt to a large bowl. Whip with an electric mixer on high speed for 5 to 10 minutes, until the butter is pale, fluffy and doubled in size. Add the cookie butter and mix on medium speed until combined. Sift the powdered sugar into the mixture about ½ cup (65 g) at a time. Mix on low, then medium, speed, making sure each addition is fully combined before adding the next. Scrape the sides and bottom of the bowl as necessary.

Then add the vanilla and ground Oreos and mix on medium, then high, speed for about 1 minute, until the frosting is light and fluffy. Transfer the frosting to a piping bag fitted with a large decorative tip.

When the cupcakes are completely cooled, pipe a generous amount of frosting onto each cupcake. Sprinkle crushed Oreos and crushed Lotus Biscoff cookies over the cupcakes and top with halved cookies (if desired), then serve!

Salted Caramel Latte Mini Cake

All my fancy coffee drinkers unite! This Salted Caramel Latte Mini Cake tastes just like the coffee drink we love. Moist and tender layers of espresso cake are made with brewed espresso and espresso powder for a rich espresso flavor. The cake layers are filled and frosted with an incredible salted caramel coffee buttercream that will truly wow you. The mini cake is topped with a glorious salted caramel drip and swirls of more salted caramel coffee buttercream. Top with espresso beans to make the cake look extra fancy! This cake is dedicated to me, and all the lattes I consumed while writing this book.

Yield: 1 (4-inch [10-cm]) three-tier cake

For the Salted Caramel Sauce
½ cup (100 g) granulated sugar
3 tbsp (42 g) unsalted butter, softened
¼ cup (60 ml) heavy cream, at room temperature
⅛–¼ tsp salt (depending on preference)
½ tsp vanilla bean paste or extract

For the Espresso Cake
1¼ cups (140 g) cake flour, spooned and leveled
1 tbsp (7 g) espresso powder
¾ tsp baking powder
⅛ tsp baking soda
¼ tsp salt
5 tbsp (70 g) unsalted butter, softened
¾ cup (150 g) granulated sugar

2 egg whites, at room temperature
1 tsp vanilla bean paste or extract
⅓ cup (80 ml) buttermilk, at room temperature
¼ cup (60 ml) brewed espresso, at room temperature

For the Salted Caramel Coffee Buttercream
¾ cup unsalted butter, softened
⅛ tsp salt
2 tsp (2 g) instant coffee, finely crushed (see Note)
1 tsp vanilla bean paste or extract
1½ cups (195 g) powdered sugar

Coffee beans, for decoration (optional)

Make the salted caramel sauce first so it has plenty of time to cool. Add the sugar to a small saucepan and heat it over medium-low heat. As the sugar is heating it will crystalize and then eventually melt down and turn golden in color. When most of the sugar has melted, but there are still a few crystalized clumps, turn the heat down to low so the melted sugar doesn't burn. Melting all the sugar should take 10 to 15 minutes.

Once the sugar has melted and turned golden in color, add the butter right away. Stir quickly until the butter is incorporated. Then add the heavy cream and stir quickly again to incorporate everything. (At this point, if you see the butter and cream start to separate from the sugar, turn up the heat to medium-low and stir vigorously to combine everything.) Add the salt and vanilla and stir to combine. Let the caramel simmer for 1 to 2 minutes to allow it to thicken a little more. Remove from the heat and allow it to cool completely.

(continued)

To make the espresso cake, preheat the oven to 350°F (177°C). Spray three 4-inch (10-cm) cake pans with nonstick spray and line the bottoms with parchment paper rounds, then set aside. In a small bowl, whisk together the cake flour, espresso powder, baking powder, baking soda and salt, then set aside. In a large bowl, cream the butter and sugar together with an electric mixer on high speed for 2 to 3 minutes, until it is fluffy.

Next, add the egg whites and vanilla and mix on medium-high speed for 1 to 2 minutes, until pale and smooth. Add in the buttermilk and half the dry ingredients to the butter mixture and combine on low, then medium, speed, scraping the sides and bottom of the bowl with a spatula as necessary. Then add the rest of the dry ingredients and the espresso. Mix on low, then medium, speed just until the batter is smooth.

Divide the batter evenly between the cake pans. Bake the cakes for 25 to 28 minutes, or until a cake tester or toothpick comes out clean from the centers. Let the cakes cool in their pans for 2 minutes, then transfer them to a cooling rack to cool completely.

To make the salted caramel coffee buttercream, add the butter, salt, instant coffee and vanilla to a large bowl. Mix with an electric mixer on high speed for 5 to 10 minutes, until the butter is pale, fluffy and doubled in size. Add ¼ cup (70 g) of salted caramel sauce and mix on medium speed until combined.

Sift the powdered sugar into the mixture ½ cup (65 g) at a time. Mix on low, then medium, speed, making sure each addition is fully combined before adding the next. Scrape the sides and bottom of the bowl as necessary. When the last addition is added, mix on high speed for about 1 minute, until the frosting is light and fluffy.

Please see page 12 for mini cake assembly instructions, using the salted caramel coffee buttercream and salted caramel sauce for a drip when indicated. Decorate with coffee beans (if using) and serve!

Note: For the frosting, add instant coffee to a baggie and crush with a rolling pin until finely ground.

PB&J Cupcakes

It doesn't get much more nostalgic than peanut butter and jelly, and while PB&J sandwiches are nothing new, PB&J Cupcakes are! These melt in your mouth peanut butter cupcakes are filled with homemade raspberry jam and topped with creamy peanut butter buttercream frosting. A drizzle of jam and a sprinkle of chopped peanuts finishes them off. They'll transport you right back to the good old days of eating PB&J as a kid!

Yield: 12 cupcakes

For the Raspberry Jam
12 oz (340 g) fresh raspberries
¾ cup (150 g) granulated sugar
1 tsp vanilla bean paste or extract

For the Peanut Butter Cupcakes
1 cup + 2 tbsp (141 g) all-purpose flour, spooned and leveled
¾ tsp baking powder
⅛ tsp baking soda
¼ tsp salt
¼ cup (56 g) unsalted butter, softened
¾ cup (150 g) granulated sugar
1 egg, at room temperature
1 egg yolk, at room temperature
1 tsp vanilla bean paste or extract
¼ cup (64 g) creamy peanut butter
½ cup (120 ml) buttermilk, at room temperature

For the Peanut Butter Buttercream
¾ cup (168 g) unsalted butter, softened
⅛ tsp salt
6 tbsp (96 g) creamy peanut butter (see Note)
1½ cups (195 g) powdered sugar
½ tsp vanilla bean paste or extract

Chopped peanuts, for decoration (optional)

Start the raspberry jam first so it has plenty of time to cool. Add the raspberries to a blender and blend until they are puréed. Strain the purée over a large saucepan to separate most of the seeds from the purée. (It's okay if some get through. Additionally, this step is optional if you don't mind all the seeds.) Add the sugar and vanilla. Heat over medium heat until the purée has thickened into a jam-like consistency and measures out to ¾ cup (180 ml). This should take 15 to 20 minutes. Remove the jam from the heat and allow it to cool completely.

To make the peanut butter cupcakes, preheat the oven to 350°F (177°C). Line a cupcake pan with 12 liners, then set aside. In a small bowl, sift together the flour, baking powder, baking soda and salt, then set aside. In a large bowl, cream the butter and granulated sugar together with an electric mixer on high speed for 2 to 3 minutes until light and fluffy. Then add the egg, egg yolk and vanilla and mix on medium-high speed for 1 to 2 minutes, until pale, smooth and slightly fluffy. Scrape the sides and bottom of the bowl with a spatula as necessary.

Next, add the peanut butter and mix on medium speed just until combined. Alternate adding the dry ingredients and the buttermilk to the butter mixture a little at a time, until each has been added completely, mixing on low, then medium, speed for each addition. Mix just until the batter is combined and smooth, scraping the sides and bottom of the bowl as necessary. Divide the batter among the 12 liners until each is about two-thirds to three-quarters full. Bake the cupcakes for 18 to 20 minutes, or until a cake tester or toothpick comes out clean from the centers. Let the cupcakes cool in the pan for 10 minutes, then transfer them to a cooling rack to finish cooling.

(continued)

To make the peanut butter buttercream, add the butter and salt to a large bowl. Whip it with an electric mixer on high speed for 5 to 10 minutes until the butter is pale, fluffy and doubled in size. Add the peanut butter and mix on medium speed until combined. Sift the powdered sugar into the mixture ½ cup (65 g) at a time. Mix on low, then medium, speed, making sure each addition is fully combined before adding the next. Add the vanilla and mix on high speed for about 1 minute, until the frosting is light and fluffy. Transfer the frosting to a piping bag fitted with a decorative tip.

Please see page 15 for filled cupcake assembly instructions, using the raspberry jam as filling and peanut butter buttercream when indicated. Sprinkle chopped peanuts on top (if using) and drizzle with leftover jam, then serve!

Note: Use Jif or a similar kind of peanut butter and not natural peanut butter. Natural peanut butter has too much peanut oil in it and can cause the frosting to split and cupcakes not to rise as well.

Brown Butter Cupcakes

Oh. My. Word. If I had to sum up these cupcakes in one word, it would be *divine*. Brown butter really is just the best and makes anything it's in ten times better. These super soft cupcakes are made with nutty and fragrant brown butter and frosted with the most delectable brown butter buttercream. To make these cupcakes even better, they're finished with a drizzle of brown sugar caramel. Each bite of cupcake truly just melts in your mouth!

Yield: 12 cupcakes

For the Brown Butter
1½ cups (336 g) unsalted butter

For the Brown Butter Cupcakes
1 cup + 2 tbsp (141 g) all-purpose flour, spooned and leveled

¾ tsp baking powder

⅛ tsp baking soda

¼ tsp salt

¾ cup (150 g) granulated sugar

1 egg, at room temperature

1 egg yolk, at room temperature

1 tsp vanilla bean paste or extract

½ cup (120 ml) buttermilk, at room temperature

For the Brown Sugar Caramel
3 tbsp (42 g) salted butter

¼ cup (55 g) brown sugar, packed

5 tbsp (75 ml) heavy cream

½ tsp vanilla bean paste or extract

Pinch of salt

For the Brown Butter Buttercream
⅛ tsp salt

1½ cups (195 g) powdered sugar

½ tsp vanilla bean paste or extract

Make the brown butter first. Add the butter to a large saucepan and heat it over medium heat. Allow the butter to melt and come to a simmer. Simmer until the butter is giving off a nutty scent and has browned, 6 to 8 minutes. Remove it from the heat. Separate out 5 tablespoons (75 ml) of brown butter and set aside to use in the cupcakes. Transfer the remaining brown butter to a heat-safe liquid measuring cup. It should measure out to just about ¾ cup (180 ml) but if it's over, remove some until it does. Let each portion of brown butter cool completely until it is room temperature and has solidified into almost the same consistency as softened butter. It will be slightly softer than regular butter.

To make the brown butter cupcakes, start by preheating the oven to 350°F (177°C). Line a cupcake pan with 12 liners. In a small bowl, sift together the all-purpose flour, baking powder, baking soda and salt, then set aside. Add the 5 tablespoons (75 ml) of cooled brown butter and granulated sugar to a large bowl and cream together with an electric mixer on high speed for 2 to 3 minutes, until it is fluffy. Add the egg, egg yolk and vanilla and mix on medium-high speed for 1 to 2 minutes more until pale and smooth. Scrape the sides and bottom of the bowl with a spatula as necessary. Add the dry ingredients and the buttermilk to the brown butter mixture a little at a time until it is all added, mixing on low, then medium, speed for each addition. Mix just until the batter is combined and smooth, scraping the sides and bottom of the bowl as necessary.

Divide the batter among the 12 liners until each is about three-quarters full. Bake the cupcakes for 17 to 20 minutes, or until a cake tester or toothpick comes out clean from the centers. Let the cupcakes cool in the pan for 10 minutes, then transfer them to a cooling rack to finish cooling.

(continued)

Make the brown sugar caramel while the cupcakes bake. Add the butter and brown sugar to a saucepan over medium heat. Bring to a simmer for 4 to 5 minutes, until the sugar is dissolved, stirring occasionally. Turn the heat down to medium-low and stir in the heavy cream. Let it simmer for 30 seconds to 1 minute. Remove it from heat and mix in the vanilla and salt. Let the caramel cool to about room temperature before using on the cupcakes.

To make the brown butter buttercream, add the remaining ¾ cup (180 ml) of cooled brown butter and salt to a large bowl. Whip the butter with an electric mixer at high speed for 5 to 10 minutes, until it's pale and fluffy. Sift in the powdered sugar ½ cup (65 g) at a time. Mix on low, then medium, speed, making sure each addition is fully combined before adding the next. Scrape the sides and bottom of the bowl as necessary. Add the vanilla and mix on high speed for about 1 minute, until the frosting is light and fluffy. Transfer the frosting to a piping bag fitted with a decorative tip.

Once the cupcakes are cooled, pipe a generous amount of brown butter buttercream onto each, then drizzle the brown sugar caramel over the top and serve!

Chocolate Chip Cookie Dough Mini Cake

For all my friends who would rather eat cookie dough than baked cookies, this cake is for you. This mini cake is composed of tender chocolate chip cake layers that are filled with edible cookie dough and a cookie dough frosting. The assembled cake is finished with a chocolate ganache drip, swirls of cookie dough frosting, and cookie dough balls. This one is definitely a decadent, showstopping dessert!

Yield: 1 (4-inch [10-cm]) three-tier cake

For the Heat-Treated Flour for the Cookie Dough and Frosting
1 cup (125 g) all-purpose flour

For the Chocolate Chip Cake
1 cup + 2 tbsp (141 g) all-purpose flour, spooned and leveled

¾ tsp baking powder

⅛ tsp baking soda

¼ tsp salt

5 tbsp (70 g) unsalted butter, softened

½ cup (100 g) granulated sugar

¼ cup (55 g) light brown sugar, packed

1 egg, at room temperature

1 egg yolk, at room temperature

1 tsp vanilla bean paste or extract

½ cup (120 ml) buttermilk, at room temperature

½ cup (100 g) mini semi-sweet chocolate chips

For the Chocolate Chip Cookie Dough
¼ cup (56 g) softened butter

¼ cup (55 g) brown sugar, packed

2 tbsp (25 g) granulated sugar

½ tsp vanilla bean paste or extract

¼ tsp salt

2 tbsp (30 ml) heavy cream

¼ cup (50 g) mini semi-sweet chocolate chips

For the Chocolate Chip Cookie Dough Frosting
½ cup (112 g) unsalted butter, softened

2 oz (56 g) cream cheese, cold

¼ cup (55 g) brown sugar

½ tsp vanilla bean paste or extract

⅛ tsp salt

1½ cups (195 g) powdered sugar

For Chocolate Ganache Drip
3 tbsp (45 ml) heavy cream

¼ cup (50 g) mini semi-sweet chocolate chips

¼ cup (50 g) mini semi-sweet chocolate chips, for decorating bottom of cake

---

Make the heat-treated flour first. Preheat the oven to 350°F (177°C). Line a baking sheet with parchment paper and sprinkle the flour over it. Bake the flour for 15 minutes, then let it cool completely.

To make the chocolate chip cake, keep the oven preheated to 350°F (177°C). Spray three 4-inch (10-cm) cake pans with nonstick spray. Line the bottoms with parchment paper rounds and set aside. In a small bowl, sift together the all-purpose flour, baking powder, baking soda and salt, then set aside. In a large bowl, cream the butter, granulated sugar and brown sugar together with an electric mixer on high speed for 2 to 3 minutes, until fluffy. Add the egg, egg yolk and vanilla and mix on medium-high speed for 1 to 2 minutes, or until the mixture is pale, smooth and slightly fluffy. Scrape the sides and bottom of the bowl with a spatula as necessary.

(continued)

Alternate adding the dry ingredients and the buttermilk to the butter mixture a little at a time, until each has been added completely, mixing on low, then medium, speed for each addition. Mix just until the batter is combined and smooth, scraping the sides and bottom of the bowl as necessary. Add the mini chocolate chips and mix on low speed until combined.

Divide the batter evenly among the cake pans. Bake the cakes for 28 to 32 minutes, or until a cake tester or toothpick comes out clean from the centers. Let the cakes cool in their pans for 2 minutes, then transfer them to a cooling rack to finish cooling.

Make the cookie dough while the cakes bake. Add the butter, brown sugar, granulated sugar, vanilla and salt to a medium bowl. Cream together with an electric mixer on high speed for 2 to 3 minutes, until fluffy. Add ¾ cup (94 g) of the heat-treated flour and heavy cream and mix on medium-low speed to combine. Add the mini chocolate chips and combine on medium-low speed. Divide into three parts. Roll the first part of the cookie dough into mini balls for the top of the cake. The other two parts will be used later between the cake layers. Set aside the cookie dough until ready to use.

Make the cookie dough frosting while waiting for the cakes to cool. Add the butter, cream cheese, brown sugar, vanilla and salt to a large bowl. Cream together with an electric mixer on high speed for 5 to 10 minutes, until pale and fluffy and the brown sugar is dissolved into the butter. Then add ¼ cup (31 g) of the heat-treated flour and combine on low, then medium, speed. Sift in the powdered sugar ½ cup (65 g) at a time. Mix on low, then medium, speed, making sure each addition is fully combined before adding the next. Scrape the sides and bottom of the bowl as necessary. When the last addition is incorporated, mix on high speed for about 1 minute, until the frosting is light and fluffy.

To make the chocolate ganache, add the heavy cream to a small bowl and microwave it for 30 to 35 seconds or heat it over the stove in a very small saucepan just until steaming, then transfer it to a small bowl. Add the chocolate chips and stir to combine the chocolate and cream together. Transfer the ganache to a piping bag. It should be slightly warm but not hot when ready to use on the cake.

Please see page 12 for mini cake assembly instructions, using the cookie dough as filling, the cookie dough frosting and chocolate ganache for a drip when indicated. Decorate with mini chocolate chips and the reserved cookie dough balls, then serve and enjoy!

Fruity Cereal Milk Cupcakes

When you were a kid, did you drink the leftover milk from your morning cereal? Was that your favorite part of your morning? Then these cupcakes are for you! Fruity cereal is soaked in milk until the milk is saturated with that yummy cereal flavor. It then gets mixed into the cupcake batter, giving the cupcakes a nostalgic flavor and the softest texture. After baking, the cupcakes are piped with cream cheese frosting full of little bits of fruity cereal. Each bite will taste just like you're having a bowl of your favorite fruity cereal!

Yield: 12 cupcakes

For the Fruity Cereal Milk
1 cup (240 ml) whole milk
1¼ cups (55 g) fruity cereal (I used Fruity Pebbles®)

For the Fruity Cereal Milk Cupcakes
1¼ cups (140 g) cake flour, spooned and leveled
¾ tsp baking powder
⅛ tsp baking soda
¼ tsp salt
5 tbsp (70 g) unsalted butter, softened

¾ cup (150 g) granulated sugar
2 egg whites, at room temperature
1 tsp vanilla bean paste or extract

For the Fruity Cereal Cream Cheese Frosting
½ cup (112 g) unsalted butter, softened
4 oz (113 g) cream cheese, cold
2 cups (260 g) powdered sugar
¼ cup (30 g) finely ground fruity cereal

Fruity cereal, for decoration (optional)

Make the fruity cereal milk first. Add the milk and fruity cereal to a bowl and allow the cereal to soak for 25 to 30 minutes. Strain the cereal from the milk. You should have ½ cup (120 ml) of cereal milk, but if it's slightly under, add more milk until it measures out to ½ cup (120 ml).

To make the fruity cereal milk cupcakes, start by preheating the oven to 350°F (177°C). Line a cupcake pan with 12 liners. In a small bowl, sift together the cake flour, baking powder, baking soda and salt, then set aside. Add the butter and granulated sugar to a large bowl and cream together with an electric mixer on high speed for 2 to 3 minutes, until it's fluffy. Add the egg whites and vanilla and mix on medium-high speed for 1 to 2 minutes, until pale and smooth.

Add the dry ingredients and the ½ cup (120 ml) of cereal milk to the butter mixture a little at a time until it is all added, mixing on low, then medium, for each addition. Mix just until the batter is combined and smooth.

Divide the batter among the 12 liners until each is two-thirds to three-quarters full. Bake the cupcakes for 17 to 20 minutes, or until a cake tester or toothpick comes out clean from the centers. Let the cupcakes cool in the pan for 10 minutes, then transfer them to a cooling rack to cool completely.

To make the fruity cereal cream cheese frosting, add the butter to a large bowl. Whip with an electric mixer on high speed for 5 to 10 minutes, until the butter is pale, fluffy and doubled in size. Add the cream cheese and mix on medium-high speed until it is thoroughly combined. Add the powdered sugar into the mixture 1 cup (130 g) at a time. Mix on low, then medium, speed, making sure the first addition is fully combined before adding the last. Scrape the sides and bottom of the bowl as necessary.

Add the finely ground fruity cereal and mix on medium speed until combined, then on high speed for about 1 minute, until the frosting is fluffy. Transfer the frosting to a piping bag fitted with a large decorative tip.

Once the cupcakes are cooled, pipe a generous amount of fruity cereal frosting onto each. Sprinkle with fruity cereal, then serve and enjoy!

Everything but the Kitchen Sink Cupcakes

These cupcakes are the salty-sweet lover's ultimate dream dessert! I'm calling these Everything but the Kitchen Sink cupcakes because they are full of so many different mix-ins. The very best and super moist dark chocolate chip chocolate cupcakes are filled with a super indulgent salted caramel-potato chip-pretzel filling. They're then frosted with salted caramel buttercream and topped with extra salted caramel sauce, mini chocolate chips, pretzels and potato chips. These cupcakes are over-the-top delicious!

Yield: 12 cupcakes

For the Salted Caramel Sauce
½ cup (100 g) granulated sugar

3 tbsp (42 g) unsalted butter, softened

¼ cup (60 ml) heavy cream, at room temperature

⅛–¼ tsp salt (depending on preference)

½ tsp vanilla bean paste or extract

For the Chocolate Chip Chocolate Cupcakes
1 cup (125 g) all-purpose flour

5 tbsp (25 g) Dutch process cocoa powder, scooped and leveled

½ tsp baking powder

½ tsp baking soda

¼ tsp salt

1 tsp espresso powder (optional)

¼ cup (56 g) unsalted butter, softened

¾ cup (150 g) granulated sugar

1 egg, at room temperature

1 egg yolk, at room temperature

1 tsp vanilla bean paste or extract

½ cup (120 ml) milk, at room temperature

¼ cup (61 g) sour cream, at room temperature

½ cup (100 g) mini semi-sweet chocolate chips

For the Salted Caramel Buttercream
¾ cup (168 g) unsalted butter, softened

⅛ tsp salt

1½ cups (195 g) powdered sugar

For the Everything but the Kitchen Sink Filling
⅓ cup (20 g) potato chips, crushed in small pieces

⅓ cup (22 g) pretzels, crushed in small pieces

Mini chocolate chips, for decoration (optional)

12 mini pretzels, for decoration (optional)

12 potato chips, for decoration (optional)

Make the salted caramel sauce first so it has plenty of time to cool. Add the granulated sugar to a small saucepan and heat it over medium-low heat. As the sugar is heating it will crystalize and then eventually all melt and turn golden in color. When most of the sugar has melted, but there are still a few crystalized clumps, turn the heat down to low so the melted sugar doesn't burn. Melting all the sugar should take 10 to 15 minutes.

Once the sugar has melted and turned golden in color, add the butter right away. Stir quickly until the butter is incorporated. Then add the heavy cream and stir quickly again to incorporate everything. At this point, if you see the butter and cream start to separate from the sugar, turn up the heat to medium-low and stir vigorously to combine everything. Add the salt and vanilla and stir to combine. Let the caramel simmer for 1 to 2 minutes to thicken a little. Then remove the caramel from the heat and let it cool completely.

(continued)

To make the chocolate chip chocolate cupcakes, preheat the oven to 350°F (177°C). Line a cupcake pan with 12 liners and set aside. In a small bowl, sift together the flour, cocoa powder, baking powder, baking soda, salt and espresso powder (if using), then set aside. Cream the butter and sugar together in a large bowl with an electric mixer on high speed for 2 to 3 minutes, until fluffy. Add the egg, egg yolk and vanilla and mix on medium-high speed for 1 to 2 minutes, or until pale, smooth and slightly fluffy. Scrape the sides and bottom of the bowl with a spatula as necessary.

Next, add the milk and sour cream and mix on medium speed until combined. The mixture will look curdled at this point, but don't worry. Add the dry ingredients to the wet ingredients a little at a time, until all has been added, mixing on low, then medium, speed for each addition. Mix just until the batter is combined and smooth, scraping the sides and bottom of the bowl as necessary. The batter will be a little thin. Add the mini chocolate chips and mix on low speed just until combined.

Divide the batter evenly among the 12 liners until each is about three-quarters full. Bake the cupcakes for 17 to 19 minutes, or until a cake tester or toothpick comes out clean from the centers. Let the cupcakes cool in the pan for 10 minutes, then transfer them to a cooling rack to finish cooling.

To make the salted caramel buttercream, add the butter and salt to a large bowl. Whip with an electric mixer on high speed for 5 to 10 minutes, until the butter is pale, fluffy and doubled in size. Add ¼ cup (70 g) of salted caramel sauce and mix on medium speed until combined. Sift the powdered sugar into the mixture ½ cup (65 g) at a time. Mix on low, then medium, speed, making sure each addition is fully combined before adding the next. Scrape the sides and bottom of the bowl as necessary.

When the last addition is incorporated, mix on high speed for about 1 minute, until the frosting is light and fluffy. Measure out the indicated amount of frosting for the filling and transfer the rest to a piping bag fitted with a decorative tip.

To make the filling, to a medium-sized bowl, add the potato chip pieces, pretzel pieces, ½ cup (90 g) of salted caramel buttercream and 2 tablespoons (35 g) of salted caramel sauce. Gently stir everything together with a spatula.

Please see page 15 for filled cupcake assembly instructions, using the everything but the kitchen sink filling and salted caramel buttercream when indicated. Decorate with extra caramel sauce, mini chocolate chips, pretzels and chips (if using), then serve!

Magic Cookie Bar Cupcakes

Graham crackers and chocolate and pecans and sweetened condensed milk and toasted coconut, oh my! These cupcakes are a play on magic cookie bars, the easy layered dessert with everything just mentioned. Here, graham cracker cupcakes are filled with a delightful and simple sweetened condensed milk-coconut-pecan filling. They're piped with a swirl of dark chocolate buttercream and topped with extra filling. To make these cupcakes extra special, garnish with a pecan, toasted coconut flakes and mini chocolate chips.

Yield: 12 cupcakes

For the Graham Cracker Cupcakes
¾ cup (94 g) all-purpose flour, spooned and leveled

1/3 cup (34 g) graham cracker crumbs, very finely ground

¾ tsp baking powder

⅛ tsp baking soda

¼ tsp salt

5 tbsp (70 g) unsalted butter, softened

¾ cup (150 g) granulated sugar

1 egg, at room temperature

1 egg yolk, at room temperature

1 tsp vanilla bean paste or extract

½ cup (120 ml) buttermilk, at room temperature

For the Coconut Pecan Filling
¾ cup (68 g) sweetened, shredded coconut

½ cup (60 g) chopped pecans

½ cup (156 g) sweetened condensed milk

For the Dark Chocolate Buttercream
¾ cup (168 g) unsalted butter, softened

⅛ tsp salt

3 oz (85 g) dark chocolate, melted and slightly cooled

5 tbsp (25 g) Dutch process cocoa powder

1½ cups (195 g) powdered sugar

2–3 tbsp (30–45 ml) heavy cream, cold

Pecans, for decoration (optional)

Mini chocolate chips, for decoration (optional)

Coconut, for decoration (optional)

To make the graham cracker cupcakes, start by preheating the oven to 350°F (177°C). Line a cupcake pan with 12 liners. In a small bowl, whisk together the flour, graham cracker crumbs, baking powder, baking soda and salt, then set aside. Add the butter and granulated sugar to a large bowl and cream together with an electric mixer on high speed for 2 to 3 minutes, until it's fluffy. Add the egg, egg yolk and vanilla and mix on medium-high speed for 1 to 2 minutes, until pale, smooth and slightly fluffy. Scrape the sides and bottom of the bowl with a spatula as necessary. Add the dry ingredients and the buttermilk to the butter mixture a little at a time until it is all added, mixing on low, then medium, speed for each addition. Mix just until the batter is combined and smooth, scraping the sides and bottom of the bowl as necessary. Divide the batter evenly among the 12 cupcake liners. Each will be about two-thirds full. Bake the cupcakes for 17 to 20 minutes, or until a cake tester or toothpick comes out clean from the centers. Let the cupcakes cool in the pan for 10 minutes, then transfer them to a cooling rack to finish cooling.

Make the coconut pecan filling while the cupcakes cool. Keep the oven preheated to 350°F (177°C) and line a baking sheet with parchment paper. Sprinkle the coconut over the parchment paper and bake it for about 8 minutes, or until it is lightly toasted. Stir it about halfway through to ensure it is toasting evenly. Once toasted, remove the coconut from the oven and allow it to cool completely. Once cooled, add the toasted coconut, chopped pecans and sweetened condensed milk to a medium bowl and stir to combine.

(continued)

To make the dark chocolate buttercream, add the butter and salt to a large bowl. Whip with an electric mixer on high speed for 5 to 10 minutes, until the butter is pale in color, fluffy, and doubled in size. Pour in the melted and slightly cooled dark chocolate and mix on medium speed until combined. Sift in the cocoa powder and mix on low, then medium, speed until combined. Sift the powdered sugar into the mixture ½ cup (65 g) at a time. Mix on low, then medium, speed, making sure each addition is fully combined before adding the next. Scrape the sides and bottom of the bowl as necessary. Add the heavy cream and mix on high speed for about 1 minute, until the frosting is light and fluffy. Transfer the frosting to a piping bag fitted with a decorative tip.

Please see page 15 for filled cupcake assembly instructions, using the coconut pecan filling and dark chocolate buttercream when indicated. (Leftover filling was used as decoration on top of the cupcakes.) Decorate with pecans, chocolate chips and coconut (if using), then serve!

Cosmic Brownie Cupcakes

Just like the brownies we grew up eating, but better! These cupcakes are a real brownie, shiny tops and all, but baked in a cupcake liner. They are super chocolaty and ultra-fudgy, just like a good brownie should be. To make them even more decadent, they're topped with a thick swirl of chocolate fudge frosting, and of course sprinkled with those iconic chocolate rainbow candy pieces to mimic Cosmic Brownies!

Yield: 12 cupcakes

For the Brownie Cupcakes

6 tbsp (48 g) all-purpose flour

½ cup (40 g) cocoa powder

⅛ tsp salt

¼ tsp espresso powder (optional)

1 cup (200 g) granulated sugar

2 eggs, at room temperature

1½ tsp (8 ml) vanilla bean paste or extract

¾ cup (126 g) semi-sweet chocolate chips, melted

½ cup (112 g) salted butter, melted

For the Chocolate Fudge Frosting

½ cup (112 g) unsalted butter, softened

⅛ tsp salt

¾ cup (126 g) semi-sweet chocolate chips, melted and slightly cooled

5 tbsp (25 g) Dutch process cocoa powder

1½ cups (195 g) powdered sugar

3–4 tbsp (45–60 ml) heavy cream, cold

Rainbow candies, for decoration

To make the brownie cupcakes, preheat the oven to 350°F (177°C). Line a cupcake pan with 12 liners. Sift together the flour, cocoa powder, salt and espresso powder (if using) in a small bowl, then set aside. To a medium-sized bowl, add the sugar, eggs and vanilla. Whisk together until smooth. Then add the melted chocolate chips and melted butter and whisk until combined. Add the dry ingredients and stir with a spatula to combine.

Scoop the dough into the prepared liners until each is about three-quarters full. The batter will be a little firm, so use a spoon or small spatula to even it out in the liners. Bake the cupcakes for 22 to 25 minutes, or until just a few crumbs come out on a cake tester or toothpick when inserted in the centers and the tops are shiny like a brownie! Let the brownie cupcakes cool in the pan for 10 minutes, then transfer to a cooling rack to finish cooling. The cupcakes will be flat like a brownie when they are cooled.

Make the chocolate fudge frosting while the brownie cupcakes are cooling. Add the butter and salt to a large bowl. Whip with an electric mixer on high speed for 5 to 10 minutes, until the butter is pale, fluffy and doubled in size. Add the melted and slightly cooled chocolate chips and mix on medium speed until combined. Sift the cocoa powder in and combine on low, then medium, speed. Then sift the powdered sugar into the mixture about ½ cup (65 g) at a time. Mix on low, then medium, speed, making sure each addition is fully combined before adding the next. Scrape the sides and bottom of the bowl as necessary. Add the heavy cream and mix on high speed for about 1 minute, until the frosting is light and fluffy. Transfer the frosting to a piping bag fitted with a decorative tip.

Once the brownie cupcakes are cooled, pipe a generous amount of chocolate fudge frosting onto each. Sprinkle with rainbow candies, then serve and enjoy!

Ruby Chocolate Mini Cake

Ruby chocolate is a fairly new chocolate to the scene, first released in 2017. This chocolate has its own unique flavor profile that I would describe as sweet, creamy and berrylike. It truly tastes like no other chocolate I've tried before, and I knew I needed to make a cake with it! Moist and tender layers of pink velvet cake are flavored with just a hint of cocoa powder, dyed a pretty pink color and then filled and frosted with ruby chocolate buttercream. The cake is then topped with a ruby chocolate ganache drip, swirls of ruby chocolate buttercream and a sprinkle of chopped ruby chocolate.

Yield: 1 (4-inch [10-cm]) three-tier cake

For the Pink Velvet Cake

1 cup + 2 tbsp (141 g) all-purpose flour, spooned and leveled

1 tbsp (5 g) natural cocoa powder

¾ tsp baking powder

⅛ tsp baking soda

¼ tsp salt

¼ cup + 1 tbsp (70 g) unsalted butter, softened

¾ cup (150 g) granulated sugar

1 egg, at room temperature

1 egg yolk, at room temperature

1 tsp vanilla bean paste or extract

½ cup (120 ml) buttermilk, at room temperature

4–6 drops pink food coloring

For the Ruby Chocolate Buttercream

¾ cup (168 g) unsalted butter, softened

⅛ tsp salt

3 oz (85 g) ruby chocolate, melted and slightly cooled

1½ cups (195 g) powdered sugar

For the Ruby Chocolate Ganache Drip

1½ tbsp (22 ml) heavy cream

1½ oz (42 g) ruby chocolate, chopped

Ruby chocolate, for decoration (optional)

To make the pink velvet cake, preheat the oven to 350°F (177°C). Spray three 4-inch (10-cm) cake pans with nonstick spray. In a small bowl, sift together the all-purpose flour, cocoa powder, baking powder, baking soda and salt, then set aside. In a large bowl, cream the butter and granulated sugar together with an electric mixer on high speed for 2 to 3 minutes, until fluffy. Add the egg, egg yolk and vanilla and mix on medium-high speed for 1 to 2 minutes, until the mixture is pale, smooth and slightly fluffy. Alternate adding the dry ingredients and the buttermilk to the butter mixture a little at a time until each has been added completely, mixing on low, then medium, for each addition. Mix just until the batter is combined and smooth. Add the pink food coloring and mix on low speed just until combined into the batter. Divide the batter evenly among the cake pans. Bake the cakes for 27 to 30 minutes, or until a cake tester or toothpick comes out clean from the centers. Let the cakes cool in their pans for 2 minutes, then transfer them to a cooling rack to cool completely.

Make the ruby chocolate buttercream while waiting for the cakes to cool. Add the butter and salt to a large bowl. Whip it with an electric mixer on high speed for 5 to 10 minutes, until the butter is pale, fluffy and doubled in size. Pour in the ruby chocolate and mix on medium speed until combined. Then sift the powdered sugar into the mixture ½ (65 g) cup at a time. Mix on low, then medium, speed, making sure each addition is fully combined before adding the next. When the last addition is added, mix on high speed for about 1 minute, until the frosting is light and fluffy.

To make the ruby chocolate ganache, add the heavy cream to a small bowl and microwave it for 20 to 25 seconds just until steaming, then transfer it to a small bowl. Add in the chopped ruby chocolate and stir to combine. Transfer to a piping bag. The ganache should be slightly warm but not hot when ready to use.

Please see page 12 for mini cake assembly instructions. Decorate with extra ruby chocolate (if using), then serve!

Cocktails & Cordials

Have your drinks and eat them too! By far the most exciting chapter lies ahead of you with treats like Champagne & Chambord Cupcakes (page 126), Piña Colada Cupcakes (page 143), White Russian Mini Cake (page 130), Mojito Cupcakes (page 139) and so much more! If you are a cocktail connoisseur, I know you will just adore these boozy creations. Each recipe will have you excited to drink, I mean, eat the next.

Because each frosting recipe in this chapter uses alcohol, they tend to be very "soft." I recommend putting the prepared frosting in the fridge for 10 to 15 minutes to help it firm up before using it on the mini cakes and cupcakes. You may have to do this a few times while assembling the mini cakes.

Champagne & Chambord Cupcakes

The Kir Royale is my all-time favorite cocktail, and I thought it deserved to be made into a cupcake! Champagne and raspberry Chambord are simmered to a thick reduction to add the most wonderful flavor to these cupcakes. After baking, the cupcakes are topped with a pretty swirl of pink Champagne and Chambord buttercream. Sparkling sugar is sprinkled over the cupcakes for a finishing touch to resemble the typical bubbles in the cocktail.

Yield: 12 cupcakes

For the Champagne and Chambord Reduction
3 cups (720 ml) Champagne
¾ cup (180 ml) Chambord or other raspberry liqueur

For the Champagne and Chambord Cupcakes
1¼ cups (140 g) cake flour, spooned and leveled
¾ tsp baking powder
⅛ tsp baking soda
¼ tsp salt
¼ cup (56 g) unsalted butter, softened
¾ cup (150 g) granulated sugar

2 egg whites, at room temperature
1 tsp vanilla bean paste or extract
¼ cup (60 ml) buttermilk, at room temperature
¼ tsp lemon zest
1–2 drops of pink food coloring (optional)

For the Champagne and Chambord Buttercream
¾ cup (168g) unsalted butter, softened
⅛ tsp salt
2½ cups (325g) powdered sugar
¼ tsp lemon zest
Sparkling sugar for topping (optional)

Make the Champagne and Chambord reduction first so it has plenty of time to cool. Add the Champagne and Chambord to a large pot and heat it over medium-high heat. Bring to a simmer, then continue to simmer for about 30 minutes, stirring occasionally, until it has reduced to ½ cup (120 ml). Let it cool completely before using.

To make the Champagne and Chambord cupcakes, preheat the oven to 350°F (177°C). Line a cupcake pan with 12 liners. In a small bowl, sift together the cake flour, baking powder, baking soda and salt, then set aside. In a large bowl, cream the butter and granulated sugar together with an electric mixer on high speed for 2 to 3 minutes, until fluffy. Next, add the egg whites and vanilla and mix on medium-high speed for 1 to 2 minutes, until pale and smooth.

Add the buttermilk and half the dry ingredients to the butter mixture and combine on low, then medium, speed. Then add the rest of the dry ingredients and ¼ cup (60 ml) of the Champagne and Chambord reduction. Mix on low, then medium, speed just until the batter is combined and smooth. Add in the lemon zest and pink food coloring (if using), then mix on low speed just until combined. Divide the batter evenly among the 12 cupcake liners. They should be about two-thirds full. Bake the cupcakes for 17 to 19 minutes, or until a cake tester or toothpick comes out clean from the centers. Let the cupcakes cool in the pan for 10 minutes, then transfer them to a cooling rack to finish cooling.

To make the Champagne and Chambord buttercream, add the butter and salt to a large bowl. Whip with an electric mixer on high speed for 5 to 10 minutes, until the butter is pale, fluffy and doubled in size. Then sift the powdered sugar into the mixture about 1 cup (130 g) at a time. Mix on low, then medium, speed, making sure each addition is fully combined before adding the next. Then add ¼ cup (60 ml) of the Champagne and Chambord reduction and lemon zest and mix until on medium, then high, speed for about 1 minute, until the frosting is light and fluffy. Transfer the frosting to a piping bag fitted with a decorative tip.

Once the cupcakes are cooled, pipe a generous amount of buttercream onto each and sprinkle with sparkling sugar (if using), then serve.

Grasshopper Cupcakes

What could be better than chocolate and creamy mint? These mint cupcakes have crème de cacao and crème de menthe mixed into the batter, giving them a pretty green hue. They're topped with a piping of white chocolate mint buttercream frosting and a sprinkle of chocolate shavings for a special touch.

Yield: 12 cupcakes

For the Grasshopper Cupcakes

1 cup + 2 tbsp (141 g) all-purpose flour, spooned and leveled

¾ tsp baking powder

⅛ tsp baking soda

¼ tsp salt

¼ cup (56 g) unsalted butter, softened

¾ cup (150 g) granulated sugar

2 egg whites, at room temperature

½ tsp peppermint extract

¼ cup (60 ml) buttermilk, at room temperature

2 tbsp (30 ml) crème de menthe, at room temperature

2 tbsp (30 ml) clear crème de cacao, at room temperature

1–2 drops green food coloring (optional)

For the White Chocolate Grasshopper Buttercream

¾ cup (168 g) unsalted butter, softened

⅛ tsp salt

2 oz (56 g) white chocolate, melted and slightly cooled

2 cups (260 g) powdered sugar

¼ tsp peppermint extract

1 tbsp (15 ml) crème de menthe

1 tbsp (15 ml) clear crème de cacao

2–4 drops green food coloring (optional)

Chocolate shavings, for decoration (optional)

To make the Grasshopper cupcakes, preheat the oven to 350°F (177°C). Line a cupcake pan with 12 liners and set aside. In a small bowl, whisk together the flour, baking powder, baking soda and salt, then set aside. In a large bowl, cream the butter and sugar together with an electric mixer on high speed for 2 to 3 minutes, until fluffy. Add the egg whites and peppermint extract and mix on medium-high speed for 1 to 2 minutes, until pale and smooth. Add the buttermilk and half the dry ingredients to the butter mixture and combine on low, then medium, speed. Then add the rest of the dry ingredients, crème de menthe and crème de cacao. Mix on low, then medium, speed just until the batter is combined and smooth. Add the green food coloring (if using) and mix on low speed just until combined into the batter. Divide the batter evenly among the 12 liners until each is about two-thirds to three-quarters full. Bake the cupcakes for 16 to 18 minutes, or until a cake tester or toothpick comes out clean from the centers. Let the cupcakes cool in the pan for 10 minutes, then transfer them to a cooling rack to cool completely.

To make the white chocolate Grasshopper buttercream, add the butter and salt to a large bowl. Whip with an electric mixer on high speed for 5 to 10 minutes until the butter is pale, fluffy and doubled in size. Add the white chocolate and combine on medium speed. Sift the powdered sugar into the mixture 1 cup (130 g) at a time. Mix on low, then medium, speed, making sure each addition is fully combined before adding the next. Then add the peppermint extract, crème de menthe, crème de cacao and green food coloring (if using) and mix on low, then high, speed for about 1 minute, until the frosting is light and fluffy. Transfer the frosting to a piping bag fitted with a decorative tip.

Once the cupcakes are cooled, pipe a generous amount of frosting onto each. Sprinkle with chocolate shavings (if using), then serve and enjoy!

Note: The green food coloring does tend to brown the cupcake edges, so I recommend using green cupcake liners so it's less noticeable.

White Russian Mini Cake

The White Russian is a delicious coffee liqueur, vodka and cream cocktail that seconds as a perfect cake flavor! Layers of coffee Kahlúa® cake are filled with sweet cream buttercream and frosted with a swirl of sweet cream and coffee buttercreams, replicating how the cocktail typically looks in the glass. The cake is then finished with a truly amazing white chocolate coffee ganache drip. This is a cake that any White Russian fan will absolutely adore!

Yield: 1 (4-inch [10-cm]) three-tier cake

For the Coffee Kahlúa® Cake
1 cup + 2 tbsp (141 g) all-purpose flour, spooned and leveled

1 tbsp (7 g) instant coffee, finely ground (see Note)

¾ tsp baking powder

⅛ tsp baking soda

¼ tsp salt

¼ cup (56 g) unsalted butter, softened

¾ cup (150 g) granulated sugar

1 egg, at room temperature

1 egg yolk, at room temperature

1 tsp vanilla bean paste or extract

¼ cup (60 ml) buttermilk, at room temperature

¼ cup (60 ml) Kahlúa

For the Sweet Cream and Coffee Buttercreams
½ tbsp (7 ml) Kahlúa

1 tsp instant coffee

¾ cup (168 g) unsalted butter, softened

⅛ tsp salt

½ cup (156 g) sweetened condensed milk

3 cups (390 g) powdered sugar

For the White Chocolate Coffee Ganache Drip
1 tbsp (15 ml) heavy cream

½ tsp instant coffee

1½ oz (42 g) white chocolate, chopped

To make the coffee Kahlúa® cake, preheat the oven to 350°F (177°C). Spray three 4-inch (10-cm) cake pans with nonstick spray and line the bottoms with parchment paper rounds, then set aside. In a small bowl, sift together the flour, finely ground instant coffee, baking powder, baking soda and salt, then set aside.

In a large bowl, cream the butter and granulated sugar together with an electric mixer on high speed for 2 to 3 minutes, until fluffy. Next, add the egg, egg yolk and vanilla and mix on medium-high speed for 1 to 2 minutes, until pale, smooth and slightly fluffy. Scrape the sides and bottom of the bowl with a spatula as necessary. Add the buttermilk and half the dry ingredients to the butter mixture and combine on low, then medium, speed, scraping the sides and bottom of the bowl as necessary. Add the rest of the dry ingredients and the Kahlúa. Mix on low, then medium, speed just until the batter is combined and smooth.

Divide the batter evenly among the cake pans. Bake the cakes for 26 to 29 minutes, or until a cake tester or toothpick comes out clean from the centers. Let the cakes cool in their pans for 2 minutes, then transfer them to a cooling rack to cool completely.

(continued)

To make the sweet cream and coffee buttercreams, add the Kahlúa and instant coffee to a small ramekin. Microwave for 10 seconds or until the instant coffee is dissolved into the Kahlúa. Then set aside to cool completely. Add the butter and salt to a large bowl. Whip with an electric mixer on high speed for 5 to 10 minutes, until the butter is pale, fluffy and doubled in size. Add the sweetened condensed milk and combine on medium speed.

Sift in the powdered sugar 1 cup (130 g) at a time. Mix on low, then medium, speed, making sure each addition is fully combined before adding the next. Scrape the sides and bottom of the bowl as necessary. When the last addition is incorporated, mix on high speed for about 1 minute, until the frosting is light and fluffy. Measure out 1 cup (180 g) of the frosting, add it to a small bowl and mix the cooled Kahlúa and instant coffee mixture into it.

To make the white chocolate coffee ganache, add the cream and instant coffee to a small bowl and microwave for 20 seconds or heat it over the stove in a very small saucepan until steaming, then transfer it to a small bowl. Add the white chocolate and stir to combine. Let it cool to room temperature before using on the cake.

Please see page 12 for mini cake assembly instructions, using the sweet cream buttercream, coffee buttercream and white chocolate coffee ganache when indicated. Fill and frost cake with the sweet cream buttercream, then swirl coffee buttercream into the final layer of frosting. Place dollops of coffee buttercream on the outside of the cake and use a cake scraper to scrape it across the cake, giving you the swirl effect, then serve!

Note: Add instant coffee to a baggie and crush with a rolling pin until finely ground.

Almond Amaretto Mini Cake

Amaretto is a fantastically delicious cordial that is just begging to be baked with. It's sweet with notes of almond and cherry and made the perfect addition to this almond mini cake. This is an Almond Amaretto Mini Cake, frosted with thick and creamy almond caramel buttercream and finished with an amaretto caramel drip. Not only is this cake pretty; it'll blow everyone away with how delicious it is!

Yield: 1 (4-inch [10-cm]) three-tier cake

For the Amaretto Caramel Sauce
½ cup (100 g) granulated sugar
3 tbsp (42 g) unsalted butter, softened
¼ cup (60 ml) heavy cream, at room temperature
⅛–¼ tsp salt
½ tsp vanilla bean paste or extract
¼ tsp almond extract
3 tbsp (45 ml) amaretto (Disaronno® was used)

For the Almond Amaretto Cake
1 cup + 2 tbsp (141 g) all-purpose flour
¾ tsp baking powder
⅛ tsp baking soda
¼ tsp salt
¼ cup (56 g) unsalted butter, softened

¾ cup (150 g) granulated sugar
1 egg, at room temperature
1 egg yolk, at room temperature
1 tsp vanilla bean paste or extract
½ tsp almond extract
¼ cup (60 ml) buttermilk, at room temperature
¼ cup (60 ml) amaretto, at room temperature (Disaronno was used)

For the Amaretto Caramel Buttercream
¾ cup (168 g) unsalted butter, softened
⅛ tsp salt
1½ cups (195 g) powdered sugar
¼ tsp almond extract

Sliced almonds, for decoration (optional)

Make the amaretto caramel sauce first so it has plenty of time to cool. Add the sugar to a small saucepan and heat it over medium-low heat. As the sugar is heating it will crystalize and then eventually melt down and turn golden in color. When most of the sugar has melted, but there are still a few crystalized clumps, turn the heat down to low so the melted sugar doesn't burn. Melting all the sugar should take 10 to 15 minutes.

Once all the sugar has melted and turned golden in color, add the butter right away. Stir quickly until the butter is incorporated. Pour in the heavy cream and stir quickly again to incorporate everything. At this point, if you see the butter and cream start to separate from the sugar, turn up the heat to medium-low and stir vigorously to combine everything together.

Add the salt, vanilla, almond extract and amaretto and stir to combine. Let the caramel simmer for 2 to 3 minutes to allow it to thicken a little more. Then remove it from the heat and refrigerate until cold. This is a thinner caramel, and it is much easier to work with when it's cold.

(continued)

To make the almond amaretto cake, preheat the oven to 350°F (177°C). Spray three 4-inch (10-cm) cake pans with nonstick spray and line the bottoms with parchment paper, then set aside. In a small bowl, sift together the flour, baking powder, baking soda and salt, then set aside. In a large bowl, cream the butter and granulated sugar together with an electric mixer on high speed for 2 to 3 minutes, until fluffy.

Add the egg, egg yolk, vanilla and almond extract and mix on medium-high speed for 1 to 2 minutes, until pale, smooth and slightly fluffy. Scrape the sides and bottom of the bowl as necessary. Add the buttermilk and half the dry ingredients to the butter mixture and combine on low, then medium, speed, scraping the sides of the bowl with a spatula as necessary. Then add the rest of the dry ingredients and the amaretto. Mix on low, then medium, speed just until the batter is combined and smooth.

Divide the batter among the cake pans. Bake the cakes for 25 to 28 minutes, or until a cake tester or toothpick comes out clean from the centers. Let the cakes cool in their pans for 2 minutes, then transfer them to a cooling rack to finish cooling.

To make the amaretto caramel buttercream, add the butter and salt to a large bowl. Whip with an electric mixer on high speed for 5 to 10 minutes, until the butter is pale, fluffy and doubled in size. Add ¼ cup (70 g) of the amaretto caramel sauce and mix on medium speed until combined. Sift the powdered sugar into the mixture ½ cup (65 g) at a time. Mix on low, then medium, speed, making sure each addition is fully combined before adding the next. Scrape the sides and bottom of the bowl as necessary. Then add the almond extract and mix on high speed for about 1 minute, until the frosting is light and fluffy.

Please see page 12 for mini cake assembly instructions, using the amaretto caramel buttercream and amaretto caramel sauce for a drip when indicated. Top with sliced almonds (if using), then serve!

Bailey's Irish Cream® Cupcakes

I mean, how could I not include a Bailey's-flavored cupcake in this chapter?! Bailey's really is the quintessential cordial and is absolutely perfect in baked goods. These cupcakes have just a touch of coffee, vanilla and chocolate flavor to mimic the flavors in Irish cream, and of course they have Bailey's mixed right into the batter. They're frosted with swirls of delectably smooth Bailey's buttercream and sprinkled with chocolate shavings. I dare you to try to eat just one!

Yield: 12 cupcakes

For the Bailey's® Cupcakes
1 cup + 2 tbsp (141 g) all-purpose flour, spooned and leveled

1 tbsp (5 g) Dutch process cocoa powder, scooped and leveled

½ tsp espresso powder

¾ tsp baking powder

⅛ tsp baking soda

¼ tsp salt

¼ cup (56 g) unsalted butter, softened

¾ cup (150 g) granulated sugar

1 egg, at room temperature

1 egg yolk, at room temperature

1 tsp vanilla bean paste or extract

¼ cup (60 ml) buttermilk, at room temperature

¼ cup (60 ml) Bailey's, at room temperature

For the Bailey's® Buttercream
¾ cup (168 g) unsalted butter, softened

⅛ tsp salt

2½ cups (325 g) powdered sugar

¼ cup (60 ml) Bailey's, at room temperature

1 tsp vanilla bean paste or extract

Chocolate shavings, for decoration (optional)

To make the Bailey's® cupcakes, preheat the oven to 350°F (177°C). Line a cupcake pan with 12 liners and set aside. In a small bowl, whisk together the flour, cocoa powder, espresso powder, baking powder, baking soda and salt, then set aside. In a large bowl, cream the butter and sugar together with an electric mixer on high speed for 2 to 3 minutes, until it is fluffy.

Next, add the egg, egg yolk and vanilla and mix on medium-high speed for 1 to 2 minutes, until pale, smooth and slightly fluffy. Scrape the sides and bottom of the bowl with a spatula as necessary. Add in the buttermilk and half the dry ingredients to the butter mixture and combine on low, then medium, speed, scraping the sides and bottom of the bowl with a spatula as necessary. Then add the rest of the dry ingredients and the Bailey's. Mix on low, then medium, speed just until the batter is smooth.

Divide the batter evenly among the 12 liners until each is about two-thirds to three-quarters full. Bake the cupcakes for 16 to 19 minutes, or until a cake tester or toothpick comes out clean from the centers. Let the cupcakes cool in the pan for 10 minutes, then transfer them to a cooling rack to finish cooling.

To make the Bailey's® buttercream, add the butter and salt to a large bowl. Whip with an electric mixer on high speed for 5 to 10 minutes, until the butter is pale, fluffy and doubled in size. Mix the powdered sugar in about 1 cup (130 g) at a time. Mix on low, then medium, speed, making sure each addition is fully combined before adding the next. Scrape the sides and bottom of the bowl as necessary. Pour in the Bailey's and vanilla and mix on low, then high, speed for about 1 minute, until the frosting is light and fluffy. Transfer the frosting to a piping bag fitted with a decorative tip.

Once the cupcakes are cooled, pipe a generous amount of Bailey's buttercream onto each. Top with chocolate shavings (if using), then serve and enjoy!

Mojito Cupcakes

Mojitos are my go-to vacation drink. The combination of lime and fresh mint leaves signals to me that I am out of the office. Here I've taken this classic cocktail and reimagined it as a fluffy and soft mint lime cupcake, with a splash of rum, and topped it with a lime mint cream cheese frosting. These cupcakes use fresh mint leaves, lime juice and lime zest to really bring out that typical mojito flavor!

Yield: 12 cupcakes

For the Mojito Cupcakes	For the Mojito Frosting
1¼ cups (140 g) cake flour, spooned and leveled	½ cup + 2 tbsp (140 g) unsalted butter, softened
¾ tsp baking powder	2 oz (56 g) cream cheese, cold
⅛ tsp baking soda	2 cups (260 g) powdered sugar
¼ tsp salt	1 tbsp (15 ml) rum
5 tbsp (70 g) unsalted butter, softened	½ tsp lime zest
¾ cup (150 g) granulated sugar	2 tsp (2 g) fresh mint leaves, finely chopped
2 egg whites, room temperature	
¼ cup (60 ml) buttermilk, at room temperature	12 lime slices, for decoration (optional)
2 tbsp (30 ml) white rum	12 mint leaves, for decoration (optional)
1 tbsp lime juice	
½ tsp lime zest	
1 tbsp (3 g) fresh mint leaves, finely chopped	

To make the mojito cupcakes, preheat the oven to 350°F (177°C). Line a cupcake pan with 12 liners and set aside. In a small bowl, sift together the cake flour, baking powder, baking soda and salt, then set aside. In a large bowl, cream the butter and granulated sugar together with an electric mixer on high speed for 2 to 3 minutes, until it is light and fluffy. Add the egg whites and mix on medium-high speed for 1 to 2 minutes, until pale and smooth. Scrape the sides and bottom of the bowl with a spatula as necessary.

Add the buttermilk and half the dry ingredients to the butter mixture. Mix on low, then medium, speed, scraping the sides and bottom of the bowl as necessary. Then add the rest of the dry ingredients, the rum, lime juice, lime zest and chopped mint. Mix on low, then medium, speed just until all is combined.

Divide the batter evenly among the liners. Each should be about two-thirds full. Bake the cupcakes for 16 to 18 minutes, or until a cake tester or toothpick comes out clean from the centers. Let the cupcakes cool in the pan for 10 minutes, then transfer them to a cooling rack to finish cooling.

To make the mojito frosting, add the butter to a large bowl. Whip on high with an electric mixer for 5 to 10 minutes, until the butter is pale, fluffy and doubled in size. Add the cream cheese and mix on medium-high speed until thoroughly combined.

Then add the powdered sugar into the mixture 1 cup (130 g) at a time. Mix on low, then medium, speed, making sure the first addition is fully combined before adding the last. Scrape the sides and bottom of the bowl as necessary. Then add the rum, lime zest, and finely chopped mint. Mix on high speed for about 1 minute, until the frosting is light and fluffy. Transfer the frosting to a piping bag fitted with a decorative tip.

When the cupcakes are completely cooled, pipe a generous amount of mojito frosting onto each. Top with a lime slice and a mint leaf (if using) and serve!

Margarita Cupcakes

Margaritas transport me to Mexico, with its beautiful sandy beaches and picturesque snorkeling. These cupcakes mimic a perfect classic margarita. Fluffy white cupcakes are made with tequila, orange liqueur, lime juice and zest to bring all the flavors of the typical cocktail. After frosting, sprinkle them with flaky sea salt for that extra margarita touch. They taste just like the real thing, and any margarita fan will adore them!

Yield: 12 cupcakes

For the Margarita Cupcakes	For the Margarita Frosting
1¼ cups (140 g) cake flour, spooned and leveled	½ cup + 2 tbsp (140 g) unsalted butter, softened
¾ tsp baking powder	⅛ tsp salt
⅛ tsp baking soda	2 oz (56 g) cream cheese, cold
¼ tsp salt	2 cups (260 g) powdered sugar
5 tbsp (70 g) unsalted butter, softened	1 tbsp (15 ml) tequila
¾ cup (150 g) granulated sugar	½ tbsp (7 ml) triple sec
2 egg whites, at room temperature	1 tsp lime zest
¼ cup (60 ml) buttermilk, at room temperature	
2 tbsp (30 ml) tequila	12 lime slices, for decoration (optional)
1 tbsp (15 ml) triple sec	Flaky sea salt, for topping (optional)
1 tbsp (15 ml) lime juice	
1 tsp lime zest	

To make the margarita cupcakes, preheat the oven to 350°F (177°C). Line a cupcake pan with 12 liners and set aside. In a small bowl, sift together the cake flour, baking powder, baking soda and salt, then set aside. In a large bowl, cream the butter and sugar together with an electric mixer on high speed for 2 to 3 minutes, until it is light and fluffy. Next, add the egg whites and mix on medium-high speed for 1 to 2 minutes, until pale and smooth. Scrape the sides and bottom of the bowl with a spatula as necessary.

Add the buttermilk and half the dry ingredients to the butter mixture. Mix on low, then medium, speed, scraping the sides and bottom of the bowl as necessary. Then add the rest of the dry ingredients, the tequila, triple sec, lime juice and lime zest. Mix on low, then medium, speed just until all is combined.

Divide the batter evenly among the liners. Each should be about two-thirds full. Bake the cupcakes for 16 to 18 minutes, or until a cake tester or toothpick comes out clean from the centers. Let the cupcakes cool in the pan for 10 minutes, then transfer them to a cooling rack to finish cooling.

To make the margarita frosting, add the butter and salt to a large bowl. Whip on high with an electric mixer for 5 to 10 minutes, until the butter is pale, fluffy and doubled in size. Add the cream cheese and mix on medium-high speed until thoroughly combined.

Then add the powdered sugar into the mixture 1 cup (130 g) at a time. Mix on low, then medium, speed, making sure the first addition is fully combined before adding the last. Scrape the sides and bottom of the bowl as necessary. Add the tequila, triple sec and lime zest. Mix on high speed for about 1 minute, until the frosting is light and fluffy. Transfer the frosting to a piping bag fitted with a decorative tip.

When the cupcakes are completely cooled, pipe a generous amount of frosting onto each. Top with a lime slice and sprinkle with flaky sea salt if you desire, then serve!

Piña Colada Cupcakes

If you like piña coladas and getting caught in the rain, these cupcakes are for you! These super soft and tender cupcakes are full of crushed pineapple, shredded coconut and rum. They're piped with a swirl of coconut pineapple buttercream and garnished with a cherry, a pineapple wedge and a cute little umbrella. These Piña Colada Cupcakes will have you thinking you've been transported straight to a tropical beach!

Yield: 12 cupcakes

For the Piña Colada Cupcakes

1 cup + 2 tbsp (141 g) all-purpose flour, spooned and leveled

¾ tsp baking powder

⅛ tsp baking soda

¼ tsp salt

5 tbsp (70 g) unsalted butter, softened

¾ cup (150 g) granulated sugar

2 egg whites, at room temperature

½ tsp vanilla bean paste or extract

1 tsp coconut extract

1/3 cup (80 ml) canned, full-fat coconut milk, at room temperature

1/3 cup (75 g) crushed canned pineapple, strained with juice reserved for frosting (press through a strainer)

¼ cup (23 g) shredded coconut

1 tbsp (15 ml) rum

For the Piña Colada Buttercream

¾ cup (168 g) unsalted butter, softened

⅛ tsp salt

2 cups (260 g) powdered sugar

3 tbsp (45 ml) pineapple juice

½ tsp coconut extract

Shredded coconut, for decoration (optional)

12 maraschino cherries, for decoration (optional)

12 pineapple wedges, for decoration (optional)

12 drink umbrellas, for decoration (optional)

To make the piña colada cupcakes, preheat the oven to 350°F (177°C). Line a cupcake pan with 12 liners and set aside. In a small bowl, sift together the flour, baking powder, baking soda and salt, then set aside. In a large bowl, cream the butter and granulated sugar together with an electric mixer on high speed for 2 to 3 minutes, until fluffy. Add the egg whites, vanilla and coconut extract and mix on medium-high speed for 1 to 2 minutes, until pale and smooth.

Add the dry ingredients and the coconut milk to the butter mixture a little at a time, until all has been added, mixing on low, then medium, speed for each addition. Mix just until the batter is combined and smooth. Add the pineapple, coconut and rum and mix on medium-low speed just until combined. Divide the batter evenly among the 12 liners until each is about two-thirds to three-quarters full. Bake the cupcakes for 18 to 21 minutes, or until a cake tester or toothpick comes out clean from the centers. Let the cupcakes cool in their pan for 10 minutes, then transfer to a cooling rack to finish cooling.

Make the piña colada buttercream while the cupcakes cool. Add the butter and salt to a large bowl. Whip it with an electric mixer on high speed for 5 to 10 minutes, until the butter is pale, fluffy and has doubled in size. Then sift the powdered sugar into the mixture 1 cup (130 g) at a time. Mix on low, then medium, speed, making sure the first addition is fully combined before adding the last. Pour in the pineapple juice and coconut extract and mix on medium speed until combined. Then mix the frosting on high speed for about 1 minute, until it is light and fluffy. Transfer the frosting to a piping bag fitted with a decorative tip.

When the cupcakes are cooled, pipe a generous amount of frosting onto each. Top with shredded coconut, a maraschino cherry and pineapple wedge (if using). Add a drink umbrella if you wish and serve.

RumChata® Cupcakes

Creamy, smooth, spiced RumChata pairs perfectly with cinnamon cupcakes. These soft and fluffy cupcakes have RumChata mixed right into the batter, and they're frosted with smooth RumChata buttercream. Add a cinnamon stick as a pretty garnish to mimic how you would serve RumChata as an after-dinner cordial.

Yield: 12 cupcakes

For the RumChata® Cupcakes

1 cup + 2 tbsp (141 g) all-purpose flour, spooned and leveled

1 tsp cinnamon

¾ tsp baking powder

⅛ tsp baking soda

¼ tsp salt

¼ cup (56 g) unsalted butter, softened

¾ cup (150 g) granulated sugar

1 egg, at room temperature

1 egg yolk, at room temperature

1 tsp vanilla bean paste or extract

¼ cup (60 ml) buttermilk, at room temperature

¼ cup (60 ml) RumChata, at room temperature

For the RumChata® Buttercream Frosting

¾ cup (168 g) unsalted butter, softened

⅛ tsp salt

2½ cups (325 g) powdered sugar

¼ cup (60 ml) RumChata, at room temperature

1½ tsp (4 g) cinnamon

½ tsp vanilla bean paste or extract

12 cinnamon sticks, for decoration (optional)

To make the RumChata® cupcakes, preheat the oven to 350°F (177°C). Line a cupcake pan with 12 liners and set aside. In a small bowl, sift together the flour, cinnamon, baking powder, baking soda and salt, then set aside. In a large bowl, cream the butter and granulated sugar together with an electric mixer on high speed for 2 to 3 minutes, until fluffy.

Add the egg, egg yolk and vanilla and mix on medium-high speed for 1 to 2 minutes, until pale, smooth and slightly fluffy. Scrape the sides and bottom of the bowl as necessary. Add the buttermilk and half the dry ingredients to the butter mixture and mix on low, then medium, speed, scraping the sides and bottom of the bowl with a spatula as necessary. Add the rest of the dry ingredients and the RumChata. Mix on low, then medium, speed just until the batter is combined and smooth.

Divide the batter evenly among the 12 liners until each is about two-thirds to three-quarters full. Bake the cupcakes for 16 to 19 minutes, or until a cake tester or toothpick comes out clean from the centers. Let the cupcakes cool in the pan for 10 minutes, then transfer them to a cooling rack to finish cooling.

To make the RumChata® buttercream frosting, add the butter and salt to a large bowl. Whip with an electric mixer on high speed for 5 to 10 minutes, until the butter is pale, fluffy and doubled in size. Mix in the powdered sugar 1 cup (130 g) at a time. Mix on low, then medium, speed, making sure each addition is fully combined before adding the next. Scrape the sides and bottom of the bowl as necessary. Then add the RumChata, cinnamon and vanilla and mix on low, then high, speed for about 1 minute, until the frosting is light and fluffy. Transfer the frosting to a piping bag fitted with a decorative tip.

Once the cupcakes are cooled, pipe a generous amount of RumChata buttercream onto each. Garnish with a cinnamon stick (if using), then serve and enjoy!

Hazelnut Frangelico® Mini Cake

This mini cake has Frangelico mixed into the batter and a bit of hazelnut extract to enhance the wonderful flavors of the liqueur. The cake's buttercream frosting is of course made with Frangelico, but also uses Nutella® to play on the hazelnut and chocolate notes in the cordial. It's finished with a milk chocolate Frangelico ganache drip and a sprinkle of hazelnuts.

Yield: 1 (4-inch [10-cm]) three-tier cake

For the Hazelnut Frangelico® Cake
1 cup + 2 tbsp (141 g) all-purpose flour
¾ tsp baking powder
⅛ tsp baking soda
¼ tsp salt
¼ cup (56 g) unsalted butter, softened
¾ cup (150 g) granulated sugar
1 egg, at room temperature
1 egg yolk, at room temperature
1 tsp vanilla bean paste or extract
½ tsp hazelnut extract (optional)
¼ cup (60 ml) buttermilk, at room temperature
¼ cup (60 ml) Frangelico®, at room temperature

For the Frangelico® Nutella® Buttercream
¾ cup (168 g) unsalted butter, softened
⅛ tsp salt
¼ cup (70 g) Nutella
2 cups (260 g) powdered sugar
2 tbsp (30 ml) Frangelico

For the Frangelico® Milk Chocolate Ganache
1 tbsp (15 ml) heavy cream
½ tbsp (7 ml) Frangelico
1½ oz (42 g) milk chocolate, chopped

Chopped hazelnuts, for decoration (optional)

To make the Hazelnut Frangelico® Cake, preheat the oven to 350°F (177°C). Spray three 4-inch (10-cm) cake pans with nonstick spray and line the bottoms with parchment paper, then set aside. In a small bowl, sift together the flour, baking powder, baking soda and salt, then set aside. In a large bowl, cream the butter and granulated sugar together with an electric mixer on high speed for 2 to 3 minutes, until fluffy. Next, add the egg, egg yolk, vanilla and hazelnut extract and mix on medium-high speed for 1 to 2 minutes, until pale, smooth and slightly fluffy. Add the buttermilk and half the dry ingredients to the butter mixture and combine on low, then medium, speed. Then add the rest of the dry ingredients and the Frangelico®. Mix on low, then medium, speed just until the batter is combined and smooth. Divide the batter between the cake pans. Bake the cakes for 24 to 27 minutes, or until a cake tester or toothpick comes out clean from the centers. Let the cakes cool in their pans for 2 minutes, then transfer them to a cooling rack to finish cooling.

To make the Frangelico® Nutella® buttercream, add the butter and salt to a large bowl. Whip with an electric mixer on high speed for 5 to 10 minutes, until the butter is pale, fluffy and doubled in size. Add the Nutella and mix on medium speed until combined. Sift the powdered sugar into the mixture 1 cup (130 g) at a time. Mix on low, then medium, speed, making sure each addition is fully combined before adding the next. Then add the Frangelico and mix on medium-low, then high, speed for about 1 minute, until the frosting is light and fluffy.

To make the Frangelico® milk chocolate ganache, add the cream and Frangelico to a small bowl and microwave for 15 to 25 seconds until steaming, then transfer it to a small bowl. Add the chopped milk chocolate. Let the chocolate stand for 1 minute, then stir to combine. Let the ganache cool to just about room temperature, stirring to ensure it cools evenly. Transfer the ganache to a piping bag once it's cooled and cut a bit of the tip off once ready to use.

Please see page 12 for mini cake assembly instructions. Decorate with chopped hazelnuts (if using), then serve!

Holiday Heart-Warmers

It's the most wonderful times of the year—in cupcake and mini cake form! Fall and Christmas are when desserts really shine, so I wanted to make sure I offered an entire chapter full of the best holiday recipes. Try Pumpkin Butterscotch Mini Cake (page 150), Caramel Crème Brûlée Cupcakes (page 154), Bourbon Pecan Pie Cupcakes (page 153) and Candy Cane Marshmallow Cupcakes (page 167). The holidays are especially the time we spend in the kitchen with those we love, and I know these recipes will bring warmth and holiday cheer to you and yours.

Pumpkin Butterscotch Mini Cake

In autumn there's nothing I love more than a good pumpkin dessert, and I think this cake is the perfect option. Layers of the moistest and most perfectly spiced pumpkin cake are filled with dreamy, incredibly smooth butterscotch buttercream. This frosting is truly the best and just glides right onto the cake. It's finished with a pretty drip of butterscotch ganache and swirls of butterscotch buttercream. One bite and you'll be hooked!

Yield: 12 cupcakes

For the Pumpkin Spice Cake
1¼ cups (140 g) cake flour, spooned and leveled

2 tsp (4 g) pumpkin pie spice

¾ tsp baking powder

⅛ tsp baking soda

¼ tsp salt

5 tbsp (70 g) unsalted butter, softened

¾ cup (150 g) granulated sugar

1 egg, at room temperature

½ tsp vanilla bean paste or extract

½ cup (124 g) canned pumpkin purée, at room temperature

¼ cup (60 ml) buttermilk, at room temperature

For the Butterscotch Buttercream
¾ cup (168 g) unsalted butter, softened

⅛ tsp salt

½ cup (100 g) butterscotch chips, melted and slightly cooled

1 cup (130 g) powdered sugar

For the Butterscotch Ganache Drip
¼ cup (50 g) butterscotch chips

1 tbsp (15 ml) heavy cream

½ tbsp honey

To make the pumpkin spice cake, preheat the oven to 350°F (177°C). Spray three 4-inch (10-cm) cake pans with nonstick spray, then set aside. In a small bowl, sift together the cake flour, pumpkin pie spice, baking powder, baking soda and salt, then set aside. In a large bowl, cream the butter and granulated sugar together with an electric mixer on high speed for 2 to 3 minutes, until fluffy. Then add the egg and vanilla and mix on medium-high speed for 1 to 2 minutes, until pale, smooth and slightly fluffy.

Add the pumpkin purée and combine on medium speed. It will look curdled, but don't worry. Alternate adding the dry ingredients and the buttermilk to the pumpkin mixture a little at a time until each has been added completely, mixing on low, then medium, speed for each addition. Mix just until combined. The batter will be thick. Divide the batter evenly among the cake pans. Bake the cakes for 26 to 29 minutes, or until a cake tester or toothpick comes out clean from the centers with just a few moist crumbs. Let the cakes cool in their pans for 2 minutes, then transfer them to a cooling rack to cool completely.

To make the butterscotch buttercream, add the butter and salt to a large bowl. Whip with an electric mixer on high speed for 5 to 10 minutes, until the butter is pale, fluffy and doubled in size. Add the melted and slightly cooled butterscotch chips and mix on medium speed until combined. Add the powdered sugar ½ cup (65 g) at a time. Mix on low, then medium, speed, making sure the first addition is fully combined before adding the last. Then mix on high speed for about 1 minute, until the frosting is light and fluffy.

To make the butterscotch ganache, add the butterscotch chips and heavy cream to a small microwave safe bowl. Microwave in 15-second intervals, stirring in between, until the chips are fully melted and mixed together with the cream. The process should take about 45 seconds. Then mix in the honey. Let the butterscotch ganache cool to just about room temperature before using on the cake.

Please see page 12 for mini cake assembly instructions, then serve and enjoy!

Bourbon Pecan Pie Cupcakes

Moist and tender bourbon cupcakes are filled with real-deal pecan pie filling. They're frosted with silky cream cheese frosting and topped with extra pecan pie filling. These cupcakes absolutely deserve a spot on your Thanksgiving table!

Yield: 12 cupcakes

For the Bourbon Pecan Pie Filling
2 tbsp (28 g) unsalted butter

¼ cup (60 ml) maple syrup

⅓ cup (74 g) brown sugar

1 tbsp (15 ml) bourbon

½ tsp vanilla bean paste or extract

¼ tsp salt

1 egg, at room temperature

½ cup (55 g) chopped pecans

For the Bourbon Cupcakes
1 cup + 2 tbsp (141 g) all-purpose flour, spooned and leveled

¾ tsp baking powder

⅛ tsp baking soda

¼ tsp salt

5 tbsp (70 g) unsalted butter, softened

¾ cup (150 g) granulated sugar

1 egg, at room temperature

1 egg yolk, at room temperature

1 tsp vanilla bean paste or extract

½ cup (120 ml) buttermilk, at room temperature

2 tbsp (30 ml) bourbon

For the Cream Cheese Frosting
½ cup (112 g) unsalted butter, softened

4 oz (113 g) cream cheese, cold

2 cups (260 g) powdered sugar

Make the bourbon pecan pie filling first so it has plenty of time to cool. Add the butter to a small saucepan and melt it over low heat. Then add the maple syrup, brown sugar, bourbon, vanilla, salt and egg. Whisk to combine. Turn up the heat to medium-low and cook the mixture for 10 to 15 minutes, stirring constantly, until thick. Remove from it from the heat. Measure out 2 tablespoons (40 g) and set aside. Transfer the rest to a bowl and allow it to cool completely. Mix the pecans into the larger portion. Set aside until ready to use in the cupcakes.

To make the bourbon cupcakes, preheat oven to 350°F (177°C). Line a cupcake pan with 12 liners and set aside. In a small bowl, sift together the flour, baking powder, baking soda and salt, then set aside. In a large bowl, cream the butter and granulated sugar together with an electric mixer on high speed for 2 to 3 minutes, until fluffy. Add the egg, egg yolk and vanilla and mix on medium-high speed until pale, smooth and slightly fluffy. Alternate adding the dry ingredients and the buttermilk to the butter mixture a little at a time, until each has been added completely, mixing on low, then medium, speed for each addition. Mix just until the batter is combined and smooth. Pour in the bourbon and mix on low speed just until combined. Divide the batter among the 12 liners until they are about two-thirds full. Bake the cupcakes for 18 to 20 minutes, or until a cake tester or toothpick comes out clean from the centers. Let the cupcakes cool in the pan for 10 minutes, then transfer them to a cooling rack to finish cooling.

Make the cream cheese frosting while the cupcakes cool. Add the butter to a large bowl and whip it with an electric mixer on high speed for 5 to 10 minutes, until it is pale, fluffy and has doubled in size. Add the cream cheese and mix on medium-high speed until all is combined. Sift in the powdered sugar 1 cup (130 g) at a time. Mix on low, then medium, speed, making sure each addition is fully combined before adding the next. Then mix on high speed for about 1 minute, until the frosting is light and fluffy. Transfer the frosting to a piping bag fitted with a decorative tip.

Please see page 15 for cupcake assembly instructions. Top the assembled cupcakes with the reserved pecan pie filling and serve!

Caramel Crème Brûlée Cupcakes

The difference between regular caramel and caramel brûlée is the slightest notes of toasty, almost burnt sugar throughout. *Brûlée* means "burnt," but this is a good burnt! These might be the most involved cupcakes in this book, but the results are so worth the extra effort! These vanilla cupcakes are filled with silky smooth vanilla pastry cream, topped with caramel brûlée buttercream, drizzled with caramel brûlée sauce and sprinkled with caramel brûlée pieces. These are truly a party in your mouth and perfect for every holiday festivity!

Yield: 12 cupcakes

For the Caramel Brûlée Sauce
½ cup (100 g) granulated sugar

3 tbsp (42 g) unsalted butter, softened

¼ cup (60 ml) heavy cream, at room temperature

⅛ tsp salt

½ tsp vanilla bean paste or extract

For the Vanilla Pastry Cream
½ cup (120 ml) whole milk

2 egg yolks

6 tbsp (75 g) granulated sugar

Pinch of salt

¾ tsp vanilla bean paste or extract

2 tbsp (16 g) cornstarch, scooped and leveled

For the Vanilla Cupcakes
1 cup + 2 tbsp (141 g) all-purpose flour, spooned and leveled

¾ tsp baking powder

⅛ tsp baking soda

¼ tsp salt

5 tbsp (70 g) unsalted butter, softened

¾ cup (150 g) granulated sugar

1 egg, at room temperature

1 egg yolk, at room temperature

1½ tsp (8 g) vanilla bean paste or extract

½ cup (120 ml) buttermilk, at room temperature

For the Caramel Brûlée Topping
½ cup (100 g) granulated sugar

For the Caramel Brûlée Buttercream
¾ cup (168 g) unsalted butter, softened

⅛ tsp salt

1½ cups (195 g) powdered sugar

Make the caramel brûlée sauce first so it has plenty of time to cool. Add the granulated sugar to a small saucepan and heat it over medium-low heat. As the sugar is heating it will crystalize and then eventually all melt down and turn golden in color. Melting all the sugar should take 10 to 15 minutes.

When all the sugar has melted, turn the heat down to low and allow it to cook for 2 minutes longer to "brûlée" it. Then add the butter. Stir quickly until the butter is incorporated. Pour in the heavy cream and stir quickly again to incorporate everything. At this point, if you see the butter and cream start to separate from the sugar, turn up the heat to medium-low and stir vigorously to combine everything.

Add the salt and vanilla and stir to combine. Remove the caramel brûlée sauce from the heat and transfer it to a bowl. Allow it to cool completely before using.

(continued)

Make the vanilla pastry cream next so it has plenty of time to cool as well. In a small saucepan, heat the milk over medium-low heat just until it's steaming. Then turn the heat down to low until ready to use. To a separate small saucepan, with the heat off, add the egg yolks, sugar, salt and vanilla and whisk until combined and a pale-yellow color. (It will be thick at first but will get smooth as you whisk.) Gradually mix in the cornstarch 1 tablespoon (8 g) at a time, making sure each addition is fully combined before adding the next.

When all the cornstarch is added, heat the mixture over medium-low heat. Whisk continuously for 2 to 3 minutes, until the sugar looks dissolved and the mixture is hot. Then turn the heat down to low. To the mixture, 2 tablespoons (30 ml) of the heated milk while stirring vigorously. Pour in the rest of the milk and stir to combine. Increase the heat to medium-low again and cook for 1 to 2 minutes, whisking continuously, until the mixture is thick and soft peaks form.

Remove the pastry cream from heat. Transfer it to a bowl and place plastic wrap directly on top of the pastry cream to prevent a skin from forming. Chill it in the fridge until completely cold. Once the pastry cream is completely cold, transfer it to a piping bag until ready to use.

For tips on troubleshooting pastry cream, see page 68.

To make the vanilla cupcakes, preheat the oven to 350°F (177°C). Line a cupcake pan with 12 liners and set aside. In a small bowl, sift together the flour, baking powder, baking soda and salt, then set aside. In a large bowl, cream the butter and granulated sugar together with an electric mixer on high speed for 2 to 3 minutes, until fluffy.

Add the egg, egg yolk and vanilla and mix on medium-high speed for 1 to 2 minutes, until pale, smooth and slightly fluffy. Scrape the sides and bottom of the bowl with a spatula as necessary. Alternate adding the dry ingredients and the buttermilk to the butter mixture a little at a time, until each has been added completely, mixing on low, then medium, speed for each addition. Mix just until the batter is combined and smooth, scraping the sides and bottom of the bowl as necessary.

Divide the batter among the 12 liners until each is about two-thirds full. Bake the cupcakes for 17 to 20 minutes, or until a cake tester or toothpick comes out clean from the centers. Let the cupcakes cool in the pan for 10 minutes, then transfer them to a cooling rack to finish cooling.

To make the caramel brûlée topping, line a baking sheet with parchment paper. Add the granulated sugar to a small saucepan and heat it over medium-low heat. As the sugar is heating it will crystalize and then eventually all melt down and turn golden in color. Melting all the sugar should take 10 to 15 minutes.

When all the sugar has melted, turn the heat down to low and allow it to cook for 2 minutes longer to "brûlée" it. Then carefully pour the brûléed sugar onto the lined baking sheet and spread it in a thin, even layer with an offset spatula. Work fast as it will quickly start to harden quickly. Let it cool completely, then break it apart using a knife or the back of a spoon. I left some larger pieces for decoration and the rest in small chunks for sprinkling over the cupcakes.

To make the caramel brûlée buttercream, add the butter and salt to a large bowl. Whip with an electric mixer on high speed for 5 to 10 minutes, until the butter is pale, fluffy and doubled in size. Add ¼ cup (70 g) of the caramel brûlée sauce and mix on medium speed until combined. Sift the powdered sugar into the mixture ½ cup (65 g) at a time. Mix on low, then medium, speed, making sure each addition is fully combined before adding the next. Scrape the sides and bottom of the bowl as necessary. Then mix on high for about 1 minute, until the frosting is light and fluffy. Transfer the frosting to a piping bag fitted with a decorative tip.

Please see page 15 for cupcake assembly instructions, using the vanilla pastry cream as filling and caramel brûlée buttercream when indicated. Top with caramel brûlée sauce and caramel brûlée pieces, then serve and enjoy!

Salted Caramel Apple Mini Cake

Coming in right behind pumpkin's spot for the best fall flavor is caramel apple. This cutie mini cake is composed of layers of soft and moist spice cake, flavored with the best fall spices like cinnamon, nutmeg and allspice. It's filled with a tender salted caramel apple filling. The cake is frosted with delightfully smooth cream cheese frosting and a beautiful drip of salted caramel. Decorate the mini cake with a caramel apple for an extra cute touch!

Yield: 1 (4-inch [10-cm]) three-tier cake

For the Salted Caramel Sauce
½ cup (100 g) granulated sugar

3 tbsp (42 g) butter, softened

¼ cup (60 ml) heavy cream, at room temperature

½ tsp vanilla bean paste or extract

⅛–¼ tsp salt

For the Spice Cake
1 cup + 2 tbsp (141 g) all-purpose flour, spooned and leveled

1½ tsp (4 g) ground cinnamon

½ tsp ground nutmeg

¼ tsp ground allspice

¾ tsp baking powder

⅛ tsp baking soda

¼ tsp salt

5 tbsp (70 g) unsalted butter, softened

½ cup (100 g) granulated sugar

¼ cup (55 g) light brown sugar, packed

1 egg, at room temperature

1 egg yolk, at room temperature

½ tsp vanilla bean paste or extract

½ cup (120 ml) buttermilk, at room temperature

For the Apple Filling
1½ cups (188 g) apples, peeled, cored and diced

For the Cream Cheese Frosting
½ cup (112 g) unsalted butter, softened

4 oz (113 g) cream cheese, cold

2 cups (260 g) powdered sugar, sifted

Caramel apple, for decoration (optional)

Make the salted caramel sauce first so it has plenty of time to cool. Add the granulated sugar to a small saucepan and heat it over medium-low heat. As the sugar is heating it will crystalize and then eventually melt down and turn golden in color. When most of the sugar has melted, but there are still a few crystalized clumps, turn the heat down to low so the melted sugar doesn't burn. Melting all the sugar should take 10 to 15 minutes.

Once all the sugar has melted and turned golden in color, add the butter right away. Stir quickly until the butter is incorporated. Then add the heavy cream and stir quickly again to incorporate everything. At this point, if you see the butter and cream start to separate from the sugar, turn up the heat to medium-low and stir vigorously to combine everything.

Add the vanilla and salt and stir to combine. Let the caramel simmer on the stove for 1 to 2 minutes to allow it to thicken a little more. Once it has become thicker, remove it from the heat and allow it to cool before using on the cake. You want it to be just barely warm when applying it to the cake so it forms thick, sturdy drips without dripping all the way down the cake.

(continued)

To make the spice cake, preheat the oven to 350°F (177°C). Spray three 4-inch (10-cm) cake pans with nonstick spray and line the bottoms with parchment paper rounds, then set aside. In a small bowl, sift together the flour, cinnamon, nutmeg, allspice, baking powder, baking soda and salt. In a large bowl, cream the butter, granulated sugar and light brown sugar together with and electric mixer on high speed for 2 to 3 minutes, until fluffy.

Add the egg, egg yolk and vanilla and mix on medium-high for 1 to 2 minutes, or until the mixture is light and smooth. Alternate adding the dry ingredients and the buttermilk to the butter mixture a little at a time, until each has been added completely, mixing on low, then medium, speed for each addition. Mix just until the batter is combined and smooth, scraping the sides and bottom of the bowl with a spatula as necessary.

Divide the batter evenly among the cake pans. Bake the cakes for 24 to 27 minutes, or until a cake tester or toothpick comes out clean from the centers. Let the cakes cool in their pans for 2 minutes, then transfer them to a cooling rack to cool completely.

To make the apple filling, add the diced apples and ¼ cup (70 g) of the salted caramel sauce to a small saucepan. Cover and heat over medium-low heat for 10 minutes, or until tender. Stir occasionally to make sure everything is getting heated evenly. Let the apples cool completely before using in the cake. The filling will be divided evenly between the first and second layer of the cake when assembling it.

To make the cream cheese frosting, add the butter to a large bowl. Whip with an electric mixer on high speed for 5 to 10 minutes, until the butter is pale, fluffy and doubled in size. Add the cream cheese and mix on medium-high speed until it is thoroughly combined. Sift the powdered sugar into the mixture 1 cup (130 g) at a time. Mix on low, then medium, speed, making sure the first addition is fully combined before adding the last. Scrape the sides and bottom of the bowl as necessary. Then mix on high speed for about 1 minute, until the frosting is light and fluffy.

Please see page 12 for how to assemble mini cakes, using the cream cheese frosting, salted caramel apple filling and salted caramel sauce for a drip when indicated. Top with a caramel apple (if using), then serve and enjoy! I decorated this cake in a semi-naked fashion, but there is enough frosting to coat the cake completely.

Sticky Toffee Pudding Cupcakes

Delectable, moist date cupcakes are filled with the most incredible buttery-brown sugar toffee sauce. They're piped to perfection with scrumptious cream cheese frosting and drizzled with extra toffee sauce.

Yield: 12 cupcakes

For the Cupcakes
¼ cup (65 g) finely chopped Medjool dates

½ cup (120 ml) water

1 cup + 2 tbsp (141 g) all-purpose flour, spooned and leveled

¾ tsp baking powder

⅛ tsp baking soda

¼ tsp salt

5 tbsp (70 g) unsalted butter, softened

¼ cup (50 g) granulated sugar

¼ cup (55 g) light brown sugar, packed

1 egg, at room temperature

1 egg yolk, at room temperature

½ tsp vanilla bean paste or extract

¼ cup (60 ml) buttermilk, at room temperature

For the Toffee Sauce
½ cup (110 g) brown sugar

6 tbsp (84 g) salted butter

½ cup + 2 tbsp (150 ml) cup heavy cream

½ tsp vanilla bean paste or extract

⅛ tsp of salt

For the Cream Cheese Frosting
½ cup (112 g) unsalted butter, softened

4 oz (113 g) cream cheese, cold

2 cups (260 g) powdered sugar

To make the cupcakes, add the chopped dates and water to a small saucepan. Simmer over medium-low heat for about 5 minutes, or until all the water is absorbed and the dates are soft and have a jammy consistency. Remove the dates from the heat and allow them to cool completely. Preheat the oven to 350°F (177°C). Line a cupcake pan with 12 liners. In a small bowl, sift together the flour, baking powder, baking soda and salt, then set aside. In a large bowl, cream the butter, granulated sugar and brown sugar together with an electric mixer on high speed for 2 to 3 minutes, until fluffy.

Add the egg, egg yolk and vanilla and mix on medium-high speed for 1 to 2 minutes, until pale and smooth. Add the cooled dates and mix on medium speed until combined. Alternate adding the dry ingredients and the buttermilk to the date mixture a little at a time, until each has been added completely, mixing on low, then medium, for each addition. Mix just until the batter is combined and smooth. The batter will be thick. Divide the batter among the 12 liners until each is about two-thirds full. Bake the cupcakes for 17 to 19 minutes, or until a cake tester or toothpick comes out clean from the centers. Let the cupcakes cool in the pan for 10 minutes, then transfer them to a cooling rack to finish cooling.

Make the toffee sauce while the cupcakes bake. Add the brown sugar and butter to a saucepan over medium heat and bring to a simmer. Simmer for 5 minutes, until the sugar is dissolved and the mixture is bubbling. Stir it occasionally. Turn the heat down to medium-low and stir in the heavy cream. Let it come to a simmer again. Simmer for 3 minutes. Remove the toffee sauce from the heat and mix in the vanilla and salt. Transfer it to a bowl and let it cool to room temperature before using.

Make the cream cheese frosting while the cupcakes cool. Add the butter to a large bowl and whip it with an electric mixer on high speed for 5 to 10 minutes, until it is pale, fluffy and has doubled in size. Add the cream cheese and mix on medium-high speed until thoroughly combined. Sift the powdered sugar into the mixture 1 cup (130 g) at a time. Mix on low, then medium, speed. Mix on high speed for about 1 minute, until the frosting is light and fluffy. Transfer the frosting to a piping bag fitted with a decorative tip.

Please see page 15 for cupcake assembly instructions. Please see page 15 for cupcake assembly instructions. Top the cupcakes with extra toffee sauce and serve!

Gingerbread Cupcakes

I couldn't have a whole chapter dedicated to holiday treats without including gingerbread! These are the absolute best gingerbread cupcakes, moist and full of Christmas spices like ginger, cinnamon and cloves, and brimming with traditional molasses flavor. They're frosted with the most delectable cream cheese frosting that truly just makes these cupcakes melt in your mouth. Garnish them with a mini gingerbread man if you wish for an extra cute touch.

Yield: 12 cupcakes

For the Gingerbread Cupcakes
1 cup + 2 tbsp (141 g) all-purpose flour, spooned and leveled

¾ tsp baking powder

⅛ tsp baking soda

¼ tsp salt

1½ tsp (3 g) ground ginger

1½ tsp (4 g) ground cinnamon

½ tsp ground nutmeg

¼ tsp ground allspice

⅛ tsp ground cloves

5 tbsp (70 g) unsalted butter, softened

¼ cup (50 g) granulated sugar

¼ cup (55 g) light brown sugar, packed

1 egg, at room temperature

1 egg yolk, at room temperature

½ tsp vanilla bean paste or extract

¼ cup (85 g) unsulfured molasses

6 tbsp (90 ml) buttermilk, at room temperature

For the Cream Cheese Frosting
½ cup (112 g) unsalted butter, softened

4 oz (113 g) cream cheese, cold

2 cups (260 g) powdered sugar

12 mini gingerbread men, for decoration (optional)

To make the gingerbread cupcakes, preheat the oven to 350°F (177°C). Line a cupcake pan with 12 liners and set aside. In a small bowl, sift together the flour, baking powder, baking soda, salt, ginger, cinnamon, nutmeg, allspice and cloves, then set aside. In a large bowl, cream the butter, granulated sugar and light brown sugar together with an electric mixer on high speed for 2 to 3 minutes, until fluffy.

Add the egg, egg yolk, vanilla and molasses and mix on medium-high speed until paler and smooth, 1 to 2 minutes. Alternate adding the dry ingredients and the buttermilk to the butter mixture a little at a time, until each has been added completely, mixing on low, then medium, speed for each addition. Mix just until the batter is combined and smooth.

Divide the batter among the 12 liners until each is about two-thirds to three-quarters full. Bake the cupcakes for 17 to 20 minutes, or until a cake tester or toothpick comes out clean from the centers. Let the cupcakes cool in the pan for 10 minutes, then transfer them to a cooling rack to finish cooling.

Make the cream cheese frosting while the cupcakes cool. Add the butter to a large bowl and whip it with an electric mixer on high speed for 5 to 10 minutes, until it is pale, fluffy and has doubled in size. Add the cream cheese and mix on medium-high speed until thoroughly combined.

Sift the powdered sugar into the mixture 1 cup (130 g) at a time. Mix on low, then medium, speed, making sure the first addition is fully combined before adding the last. Then mix on high speed for about 1 minute, until the frosting is light and fluffy. Transfer the frosting to a piping bag fitted with a decorative tip.

When the cupcakes are completely cooled, pipe a generous amount of frosting on to each. Garnish with a mini gingerbread man (if using), and serve!

Maple Bacon Cupcakes

These literally taste like a delicious stack of pancakes with a side of bacon. If you love that sweet and salty combination, you will adore these cupcakes. The most tender maple cupcakes, made with real maple syrup, have chopped bacon mixed right into the batter. After baking they're topped with creamy maple cream cheese frosting. Garnish each cupcake with a mini slice of bacon, bacon bits and a drizzle of maple syrup for extra indulgence.

Yield: 12 cupcakes

For the Maple Bacon Cupcakes

1 cup + 2 tbsp (141 g) all-purpose flour, spooned and leveled

¾ tsp baking powder

⅛ tsp baking soda

¼ tsp salt

5 tbsp (70 g) unsalted butter, softened

½ cup + 2 tbsp (125 g) granulated sugar

1 egg, at room temperature

1 egg yolk, at room temperature

1 tsp vanilla bean paste or extract

½ cup (120 ml) buttermilk, at room temperature

2 tbsp (30 ml) maple syrup

¼ cup (30 g) maple bacon, cooked and finely chopped (3–4 slices)

For the Maple Cream Cheese Frosting

½ cup (112 g) unsalted butter

3 oz (85 g) cream cheese, cold

2 cups (260 g) powdered sugar

2 tbsp (30 ml) maple syrup

Finely chopped cooked bacon, for decoration (optional)

12 cooked bacon slices, for decoration (optional)

Maple syrup, for drizzling (optional)

To make the maple bacon cupcakes, preheat oven to 350°F (177°C). Line a cupcake pan with 12 liners and set aside. In a small bowl, sift together the flour, baking powder, baking soda and salt, then set aside. In a large bowl, cream the butter and granulated sugar together with an electric mixer on high speed for 2 to 3 minutes, until fluffy. Add the egg, egg yolk and vanilla and mix on medium-high speed for 1 to 2 minutes, until pale, smooth and slightly fluffy. Scrape the sides and bottom of the bowl with a spatula as necessary.

Alternate adding the dry ingredients and the buttermilk to the butter mixture a little at a time, until each has been added completely, mixing on low, then medium, speed for each addition. Mix just until the batter is combined and smooth, scraping the sides and bottom of the bowl as necessary. Then add in the maple syrup and chopped bacon pieces and mix on low speed just until evenly dispersed through the batter.

Divide the batter among the 12 liners until each is about two-thirds to three-quarters full. Bake the cupcakes for 18 to 20 minutes, or until a cake tester or toothpick comes out clean from the centers. Let the cupcakes cool in the pan for 10 minutes, then transfer them to a cooling rack to cool completely.

Make the maple cream cheese frosting while the cupcakes cool. Add the butter to a large bowl and whip it with an electric mixer on high speed for 5 to 10 minutes, until it is pale, fluffy and has doubled in size. Add the cream cheese and mix on medium-high speed until thoroughly combined. Sift the powdered sugar into the mixture 1 cup (130 g) at a time. Mix on low, then medium, speed, making sure the first addition is fully combined before adding the last. Then add the maple syrup and mix on high speed for about 1 minute, until the frosting is light and fluffy. Transfer the frosting to a piping bag fitted with a decorative tip.

When the cupcakes are completely cooled, pipe a generous amount of frosting on to each. Sprinkle with bacon pieces and top with a small slice of bacon (if using). Drizzle extra maple syrup (if desired) over the top and serve!

Candy Cane Marshmallow Cupcakes

Soft and fluffy peppermint cupcakes are filled with ooey-gooey peppermint marshmallow filling. They're piped with a pretty swirl red-and-white peppermint marshmallow buttercream to look like a candy cane. Top them with a mini candy cane and mini marshmallows for extra Christmas cuteness.

Yield: 12 cupcakes

For the Peppermint Cupcakes
1¼ cups (140 g) cake flour, spooned and leveled

¾ tsp baking powder

⅛ tsp baking soda

¼ tsp salt

5 tbsp (70 g) unsalted butter, softened

¾ cup (150 g) granulated sugar

2 egg whites, at room temperature

1 tsp vanilla bean paste or extract

½ tsp peppermint extract

½ cup (120 ml) buttermilk, at room temperature

For the Marshmallow Peppermint Frosting
¾ cup (168 g) unsalted butter, softened

1½ cups (150 g) marshmallow fluff

1½ cups (195 g) powdered sugar

½ tsp peppermint extract

Red food coloring

For the Marshmallow Peppermint Filling
1¼ cups (125 g) marshmallow fluff

⅛ tsp peppermint extract

12 mini candy canes, for decoration (optional)

Mini marshmallows, for decoration (optional)

To make the peppermint cupcakes, preheat the oven to 350°F (177°C). Line a cupcake pan with 12 liners and set aside. In a small bowl, sift together the cake flour, baking powder, baking soda and salt, then set aside. In a large bowl, cream the butter and granulated sugar together with an electric mixer on high speed for 2 to 3 minutes, until it is light and fluffy.

Add the egg whites, vanilla and peppermint extract and mix on medium-high speed for 1 to 2 minutes, until pale and smooth. Alternate adding the dry ingredients and the buttermilk to the butter mixture a little at a time, until each has been added completely, mixing on low, then medium, speed for each addition. Mix just until the batter is combined and smooth. Divide the batter evenly among the 12 liners until each is about two-thirds to three-quarters full. Bake the cupcakes for 16 to 18 minutes, or until a cake tester or toothpick comes out clean from the centers. Let the cupcakes cool in the pan for 10 minutes, then transfer them to a cooling rack to finish cooling.

To make the marshmallow peppermint frosting, add the butter to a large bowl. Whip with an electric mixer on high speed for 5 to 10 minutes, until the butter is pale, fluffy and doubled in size. Add the marshmallow fluff and mix on medium speed until it is thoroughly combined. Sift the powdered sugar into the mixture ½ cup (65 g) at a time. Mix on low, then medium, speed, making sure each addition is fully combined before adding the next. Add the peppermint extract and mix on high speed for about 1 minute, until the frosting is light and fluffy.

Remove ½ cup (about 105 g) of the frosting and add it to a small bowl. Mix a few drops of red food coloring into the frosting until it's as red as you wish. Add about half of the white frosting to a piping bag fitted with a decorative tip. Hollow out a bit of the center by pushing the white frosting up the sides of the bag using a small spatula. Add the red frosting to the center of the bag, then close it in with more white frosting.

For the marshmallow peppermint filling, add the marshmallow fluff and peppermint extract to a small bowl. Mix until the extract is combined into the fluff. Transfer it to a piping bag and cut off a bit of the tip when ready to use.

Please see page 15 for cupcake assembly instructions. Garnish with mini candy canes and mini marshmallows (if using), then serve!

Apple Butter Cupcakes

These quick and easy fall cupcakes will bring all the warm autumn spices and smells right into your kitchen. Soft and fluffy spiced cupcakes, with cinnamon, nutmeg and allspice, have apple butter mixed right into the batter. After baking they're frosted with swirls of creamy and delicious spiced cream cheese frosting. Drizzle extra apple butter on top for more fall deliciousness!

Yield: 12 cupcakes

For the Apple Butter Cupcakes

1 cup + 2 tbsp (141 g) all-purpose flour, spooned and leveled

2 tsp (6 g) ground cinnamon

½ tsp ground nutmeg

¼ tsp ground allspice

¾ tsp baking powder

⅛ tsp baking soda

¼ tsp salt

5 tbsp (70 g) unsalted butter, softened

½ cup (100 g) granulated sugar

¼ cup (55 g) light brown sugar, packed

1 egg, at room temperature

1 egg yolk, at room temperature

1 tsp vanilla bean paste or extract

¼ cup (76 g) apple butter, at room temperature

¼ cup (60 ml) buttermilk, at room temperature

For the Spiced Cream Cheese Frosting

½ cup (112 g) unsalted butter, softened

4 oz (113 g) cream cheese, cold

2 cups (260 g) powdered sugar

½ tsp ground cinnamon

¼ tsp ground nutmeg

⅛ tsp ground allspice

Apple butter, for drizzling over the cupcakes (optional)

To make the apple butter cupcakes, preheat the oven to 350°F (177°C). Line a cupcake pan with 12 liners and set aside. In a small bowl, whisk together the flour, cinnamon, nutmeg, allspice, baking powder, baking soda and salt, then set aside. In a large bowl, cream the butter, granulated sugar and light brown sugar together with an electric mixer on high speed for 2 to 3 minutes, until it is light and fluffy.

Add the egg, egg yolk and vanilla and mix on medium-high speed for 1 to 3 minutes, until pale and smooth. Then add the apple butter and mix on medium speed until combined. The batter may look a little curdled at this point, but don't worry. Alternate adding the dry ingredients and the buttermilk to the butter mixture a little at a time, until each has been added completely, mixing on low, then medium, speed for each addition. Mix just until the batter is combined and smooth.

Divide the batter evenly among the 12 liners until each is about two-thirds full. Bake the cupcakes for 17 to 20 minutes, or until a cake tester or toothpick comes out clean from the centers. Let the cupcakes cool in the pan for 10 minutes, then transfer them to a cooling rack to finish cooling.

To make the spiced cream cheese frosting, add the butter to a large bowl. Whip with an electric mixer on high speed for 5 to 10 minutes, until the butter is pale, fluffy and doubled in size. Add the cream cheese and mix on medium-high speed until it is thoroughly combined. Sift in the powdered sugar 1 cup (130 g) at a time. Mix on low, then medium, speed, making sure each addition is fully combined before adding the next. Add the cinnamon, nutmeg and allspice. Mix on medium-low, then high, speed for about 1 minute, until the frosting is light and fluffy. Transfer the frosting to a piping bag fitted with a decorative tip.

When the cupcakes are cooled, pipe a generous amount of frosting onto each cupcake. Drizzle extra apple butter (if using) over the tops, then serve!

Spiced Chai Mini Cake

Chai in autumn is just the best. The smell of warm chai tea brings warmth to the soul and gives you that "ahh" feeling. This chai cake is made with steeped chai tea milk and a plethora of warm fall spices, like cardamon, nutmeg, allspice and cinnamon to bring all the chai flavor. The cake is frosted with a delightful chai cream cheese frosting for the ultimate autumn treat. Each bite will make you feel all warm inside.

Yield: 1 (4-inch [10-cm]) three-tier cake

For the Chai Cake
¾ cup (180 ml) milk

4 chai tea bags

1 cup + 2 tbsp (141 g) all-purpose flour, spooned and leveled

¾ tsp baking powder

⅛ tsp baking soda

¼ tsp salt

1½ tsp (4 g) ground cinnamon

¼ tsp ground ginger

½ tsp ground cardamom

¼ tsp ground nutmeg

¼ tsp ground allspice

⅛ tsp ground cloves

5 tbsp (70 g) unsalted butter, softened

½ cup (100 g) granulated sugar

¼ cup (55 g) light brown sugar, packed

1 egg, at room temperature

1 egg yolk, at room temperature

½ tsp vanilla bean paste or extract

For the Chai Cream Cheese Frosting
½ cup (112 g) unsalted butter, softened

4 oz (114 g) cream cheese, cold

2 cups (260 g) powdered sugar, sifted

½ tsp cinnamon

⅛ tsp ground ginger

¼ tsp ground cardamom

⅛ tsp ground nutmeg

⅛ tsp ground allspice

Pinch of ground cloves

Star anise, for decorating (optional)

Cinnamon sticks, for decorating (optional)

To make the chai cake, add the milk to a small pot and bring to a boil. Once boiling, remove the milk from the heat and pour into a heat-safe measuring cup. Add the tea bags and allow them to steep in it until room temperature, about 30 minutes. Squeeze excess milk out of the bags. Make sure the chai milk measures out to ½ cup (120 ml). If it's under, top with more chilled milk and set aside until ready to use.

Preheat the oven to 350°F (177°C). Spray three 4-inch (10-cm) cake pans with nonstick spray and line the bottoms with parchment paper rounds, then set aside. In a small bowl, sift together the flour, baking powder, baking soda, salt, cinnamon, ginger, cardamom, nutmeg, allspice and cloves then set aside. In a large bowl, cream the butter, granulated sugar and light brown sugar together with an electric mixer on high speed for 2 to 3 minutes, until fluffy.

(continued)

Add the egg, egg yolk and vanilla and mix on medium-high speed for 1 to 2 minutes, until pale and smooth. Scrape the sides and bottom of the bowl with a spatula as necessary. Alternate adding the dry ingredients and the chai milk to the butter mixture a little at a time, until each has been added completely, mixing on low, then medium, speed for each addition. Mix just until the batter is combined and smooth, scraping the sides and bottom of the bowl as necessary.

Divide the batter among the cake pans. Bake the cakes for 27 to 30 minutes, or until a cake tester or toothpick comes out clean from the centers. Let the cakes cool in their pans for 2 minutes, then transfer them to a cooling rack to finish cooling.

To make the chai cream cheese frosting, add the butter to a large bowl and whip it with an electric mixer on high speed for 5 to 10 minutes, until pale in color, fluffy and has doubled in size. Add the cream cheese and mix on medium-high speed until thoroughly combined.

Sift the powdered sugar into the mixture 1 cup (130 g) at a time. Mix on low, then medium, speed, making sure the first addition is fully combined before adding the last. Scrape the sides and bottom of the bowl as necessary. Add the cinnamon, ginger, cardamom, nutmeg, allspice and cloves and combine on medium speed. Once combined, mix the frosting on high speed for about 1 minute, until fluffy and smooth.

Please see page 12 for mini cake assembly instructions, using the chai cream cheese frosting when indicated. Decorate with star anise and cinnamon sticks (if using), then serve and enjoy!

About the Author

Ginny Dyer is the creator of In Bloom Bakery, a baking blog with beautiful photographs that equips home bakers with elevated dessert recipes. Ginny's passion for baking started at a young age, when she was constantly in the kitchen experimenting with different ingredients and learning the foundations of baking from her mother. She now uses her baking talents to share delicious dessert recipes in the hope that they bring joy and happiness to others.

She currently lives in beautiful, sunny Florida with her husband and fur babies. She loves the Lord Jesus and is so thankful for the beautiful life He's given her.

Acknowledgments

My Lord and Savior, Jesus Christ, without whom I'd be dead in my sins and completely lost in this world. He redeemed me, turned my life around and now allows me to use the creativity He's given me to bring Him glory. I'm so thankful for every opportunity the Lord has given me and that I get to spend the rest of my life loving Him and bringing Him glory. May this book reflect Jesus and not me.

Kevin, my husband and support system. Thank you for always telling me to pursue my dreams and for believing in me when I am so hard on myself. Thank you for trying every single recipe in this book and for always telling me you are proud of me. It can be easy for me to get caught up in just going through the motions of creating recipes and photographing them, but your encouragement makes me feel so seen and like what I'm doing is actually meaningful. (Also thank you for always helping me with the tremendous amount of dishwashing that comes along with this career. Hehe.) I love you, Kev.

Trisha, my wonderful mama. Thank you for helping me learn how to bake and for encouraging me constantly through my baking and blogging endeavors. You are the reason I fell in love with baking, and without you I truly don't think I would be doing what I am or be the woman I am today. You are one of a kind, and I hope to be as good of a mother as you one day.

Ray, my dad. Thank you for encouraging me from the start of my blogging career by telling me things like "You can be the next Pioneer Woman." You believed in me and made me feel like I could really do this whole blogging career thing at a time when I questioned every step I was making.

Jamie, my stepmom and creative help. Thank you for brainstorming the initial recipe flavors with me when I first embarked on this journey. You have a knack for seeing the world through a colorful, fun, creative lens unlike anyone else I know.

Bill, my stepdad. Thank you for always cheering me on and giving me an ego boost. Your spontaneous check-ins with me really helped me to feel loved and supported.

Kori, my best friend. To think all those years playing in the kitchen as kids turned into this. Thank you for helping spark my creativity when I was young and being here for me always. Thank you for checking in on me through this whole process and for your encouragement. I love you, bestie.

Katie, my best buddy. Thank you for encouraging me from the beginning to write this book. Your kind words about my attention to detail gave me confidence to move forward and stuck in my mind through this whole process. I'm so thankful for your friendship.

Maggie, my sister in Christ. Thank you for praying for me throughout this journey and keeping me accountable to what's most important: the Lord. I easily got my priorities sidetracked while working on this, and your encouragement to keep staying in the Word helped me tremendously. I'm so grateful to have a friend like you.

Stephanie of Stephanie's Sweet Treats, my blogging best friend. Thank you for encouraging me weekly and sometimes daily through the end of this process. Your kindness means the world to me and gave me a lift in spirt to finish this thing.

My In Bloom Bakery friends. Thank you for following along with me. I would not be where I am today without your support. It truly makes my entire day when I see that you made one of my recipes and that you and your family loved it. I am so happy that I get to be a small part of something that makes you smile. Thank you for being here and for all the support you have shown me. I cannot wait to see what we will bake together over the years to come.

Page Street Publishing Company. Thank you for allowing me the opportunity to publish my own cookbook. I never imagined being able to do this so early in my career, and you gave me that chance. A lifelong dream come true, thank you from the bottom of my heart. Emily, Meg and Emma, thank you for working with me and putting together such a lovely book.

Index